W9-BKJ-238

DEDICATION

To my daughter, Brittany, may you always play.

In honor of those fighting or living with cancer, a portion of royalties from this book will be donated by the author to the Lance Armstrong Foundation.

ACKNOWLEDGMENTS

Many thanks to the following people who provided continual support during the research and writing of this book: to Greg and Brittany Long, my constant SAG wagon in life, my little family—dad, Amy, and Mike. To my editor, Deb Werksman, and my literary agent, Elizabeth Pomada, for their wise words and inspiration; my talented book designer of my first book and again for this book, Tressa Minervini; my publicist, Megan Casper, and her associates; the marketing and sales force at Sourcebooks, including Pat Soderberg; and my publisher, Dominique Raccah, for believing in the *Permission Books* series. To all my new writer friends, Harriet Freiberger and the Art Depot writing group, and not so new writer friends, I thank you for your ongoing enthusiasm, especially my writing partner, Elizabeth Bartasius. I also want to thank all of my readers. Special thanks to reference librarian Alysa Selby of the Bud Werner Memorial Library for her incredible research and assistance on the images in this book; to Chris Hermann for the last-minute research deadline; and to Joe Kboudi and Kate Hanley at *All That Jazz* for their diverse musical insight. And lastly to all of the girls and women of Steamboat Springs, Colorado, where play is as natural in their days as eating and sleeping. I am still learning.

CONTENTS

INTRODUCTION

Most people live and die with their music
still unplayed. They never dare to try.
—Katharine Hepburn (b.1907)

Most Americans, especially women, do not play enough. In our busy modern society, there appears to be no room in our lives to invite play in. Many women are worn down by the requirements of being wife, mother, boss, and employee. With so much time over the years dedicated to others, we neglect spending time to develop and nurture our authentic selves. We need to recognize that some element of play needs to be a regular feature of our lives, not just a guest appearance on vacations, at the holidays, or waiting for retirement. However, many have decided that the notion of fun should be dismissed as child's play, or that time absorbed by pure levity is not important anymore.

The real tragedy is that American women either have no time to play or have forgotten how. As a result, many live life from the shoulders up, neglecting and ignoring their bodies, while those not happy with their size and shape spend enormous amounts of time, energy, and money trying to fix themselves.

To be truly in balance, the mind and body must dance together. When engaged in sports, outdoor games, or activities, movement is required, all in the name of fun. The mind, too, craves fun and games, such as puzzles, card and board games, hobbies, or arts and crafts. Creativity, displayed through artistic or musical expression, on the stage or the written page, can also provide the mental stimulation and challenge that housework and paperwork cannot.

Why is including fun and play in your days so important?

Watch children or pets at play—it is all for fun.

Ask any professional athlete, author, artist, or musician. Would they still play for free? "Of course" will be the resounding answer. This is their secret—those truly happy with their lives have a passion.

Play is fulfilling, energizing, and life-sustaining. This is the message that women need to hear repeatedly. Put some play back into your life. Be the model of what is important in life. Do not just talk about it, but actually play—every day.

In a nationwide survey I conducted for this book, more than two hundred American women gave interesting and honest answers to the question: "What is play?"

Play to me is any activity that gets you motivated, raises your heart rate, and you enjoy.
—Jamie Streeter, Grand Junction, Colorado

Many women emphasized the importance of playing sports, whether competing or participating just for fun. These weekend and professional athletes are proud of their hard-earned muscles, mastered skills, and abundant source of energy. Those who played since they were little girls listed the many positive characteristics and lifetime skills developed as a sportswoman as well as the added benefit of being in good health.

*Play is the feeling of extreme joy in my heart in whatever
I am doing. I could not live without that joy.*

—Donna Mass, Montebello, California

The artists who responded—craftswomen, writers, and musicians—also expressed how creative play is so crucial to their lives—the act of creating makes them whole. They are in a constant search for any type of new medium, technique, or idea that allows them to create with their hands and adds joy to their days.

Others spoke of hobbies or collecting; they cherished their time with their passion and the profound knowledge of their subject, which accumulated as a result. Still others said they reserved their creative time for pure appreciation of the arts, attending shows and performances, reading about their interest, and traveling wherever they could to learn more about their favorite artist, musician, dancer, or author. They loved the learning, the exploration, and the traveling.

Some of these women announced that they were now painting, writing, or playing an instrument rather than just observing how it is done. While several aspired to public recognition for their art, others were happy just to have this time in their lives for self-expression. All of the women surveyed had the same message for those not playing or not playing enough; Alisa Comstock from Del Rio, Texas, summed it up best: "Play is super-important—all people should play."

Play is anything you do that makes
you smile and feel better than before.
—Elise Andres, Chapel Hill, North Carolina

Kudos to you if you are one of those women who have always played. This is your guidebook to find more ways and new ideas to reach farther in your quest for self-fulfillment.

For those women who have recently returned to this healthy habit of playing—brava! And for those wise women who started to play later in life and continue no matter what the passing calendar year reports, we should applaud their dedication and tenacity, and then decide to join these active and creative women.

For all busy women who want to dedicate more time to playing, to participate without guilt and with the support of those closest to them, may the bribes, charms, and tricks within this book permit you to do just that.

This book is also written for those who desire to return to a sport or an artistic endeavor once loved as a young girl, but that now could use a nudge. Motivational tips, reasons to play, and time-management strategies are offered to help you play well and often, and to rediscover that enthusiastic spirit who once believed in all of her dreams.

For those women who have stopped or who never have played, this is your invitation to try. You deserve to be active and to be creative. Give yourself the time to have fun, laugh out loud, and smile from within. It is worth the journey. It is worth your time. Within these pages, may you find inspiration, encouragement, and permission to play.

Ecstasy
by Maxfield Parrish

CHAPTER ONE

Women Who Play Wholeheartedly

AND WITHOUT PERMISSION

Dance as though no one is watching you,
love as though you have never been hurt before,
sing as though no one can hear you,
live as though heaven is on earth.
—*Unknown*

Those little girls labeled "tomboy," "free spirit," or "artsy," have always played—released to do whatever any little boy was allowed to do. These women grew up to become athletes, artisans, and musicians, and whether they played purely for the fun of it or entered the professional world, they continue to celebrate play as adults.

I was just a little tomboy just trying to keep up with the
eight boys in town of the thirty-five people in Triumph, Idaho.
—*Picabo Street (b. 1971), 1998 Olympic Gold Super G, 1996 World*
Championships Gold Downhill, 1994 Olympic Silver Downhill

Rediscover that young girl inside you who had a wonderful passion for life and an undying curiosity for everything, or the young artist or musician who just could not stop playing. During this time, we believed our bodies to be strong, capable, and ready to conquer anything we wanted to do, be it creative or physical. Our play inspired us to be our best. We played and learned, sometimes failing and other times succeeding, but always willing to give it a try.

This year, find a new physical outlet through sports, or explore the wonders of the arts to refill your spirit. Pick up a baseball bat, golf club, or paintbrush. Start your journey to discover what type of play brings you happiness.

Follow the example of these brave women who have embraced play and enjoyed it without guilt:

- All-American softball player Donna Lopiano (b. 1946) played four different positions: pitcher, shortstop, and first and second base for the Raybestos Brakettes in Stratford, Connecticut, from the age of sixteen to nineteen. Today, she is the executive director of the Women's Sports Foundation.
- Renowned artist Beatrice Wood played all of her life. Born in 1893, she was active in her arts—ceramics, pottery, and photography—until her death at 105 years of age.
- Althea Gibson (b. 1927), the first African-American athlete to win Wimbledon, won in 1957.
- Wilma Rudolph (1940–1994), stricken with polio, was told by doctors she would never walk, let alone run. Due to her sheer determination and her mother's unconditional support, in 1960 she became the first woman to win three Olympic gold medals: 100 meters, 200 meters, and 4 x 100 meter relay.

- Susan Butcher (b. 1956), four-time winner of the Iditarod, is also a mother, wife, businesswoman, and animal lover, and has been called the "best competitive dogsled racer in the universe." The annual race takes her and her team of dogs across 1,152 miles of Alaska's coldest terrain, enduring 100 mph winds, blizzards, snow blindness, wild animals, thin ice, sleep deprivation, and avalanches.
- Karen Thorndike (b. 1942) was the first American woman to sail solo around the world—thirty-three thousand miles—crossing the most treacherous waters on earth in 1998, including the five great capes: South America's Cape Horn, South Africa's Cape of Good Hope, Australia's Cape Leeuwin, Tasmania's South East Cape, and Southwest Cape off the coast of New Zealand.
- All-American athlete "Babe" Mildred Didrikson Zaharias (1911–1956) established the Ladies Professional Golf Association in 1948.
- In 1967, Kathcrine Switzer (b. 1947) registered in the men-only Boston Marathon as K. Switzer and then ran the course in a dress to show that women were capable of handling the physical and mental demands of a 26.1-mile race. The Boston Marathon was finally opened to women five years later. The all-men New York City Marathon only permitted women in 1974. Switzer raced—wearing a dress again!

During this time of self-discovery in play, the true you will emerge. Do whatever your body and mind keeps asking you to do. If your internal voice says, "Paint," do it. If it tells you, "Hike," get outside. If it suggests, "Swim," go today. Do not wait for the weekend, your vacation, or retirement. Invite play into your life and engage your mind and body together once again.

Growth comes when the decision is made to listen to the desires of your own true heart, however modest to start with, take time to play—every day. Any time you can allocate to play is enough—even just thinking about your art can be fulfilling in days you cannot get to it. Do what you can to fit your play into a few stolen moments.

Why do I play? It establishes a sense of well-being and self-satisfaction.
—Gina M. Schiappa, Atlanta, Georgia

The results of your continual effort for self-fulfillment will be a healthier body and a clearer mind. In addition to mastering a new skill or accomplishing a goal, a calming sense of peace will be yours each day from living fully and completely. Listen to yourself. You are right.

COURAGE

Sometimes when venturing into the realm of the unknown or returning to an activity very distant from our recent memory, it helps to start with small steps. Reach for a biography of an athlete or artist whom you admire, or pick up a magazine on your new interest. The local paper is always sharing accounts of those who moved their dream into action. Be inspired by their successes. Let their stories motivate your spirit to do, to be.

> *Courage is like a muscle; we strengthen it with use.*
> —Ruth Gordon (1896–1985)

Promise yourself to accept the challenge to rediscover fun, or reach deeper into your passion if you are already playing. Tell yourself, "I have the strength to do whatever physical and creative challenges I dream of." This power to try, to do, and to become is inside all of us. You deserve this time to discover your passion and grow from it.

> *Whatever you can do or dream you can, begin it.*
> *Boldness has genius, power, and magic in it.*
> —Johann Wolfgang Goethe (1749–1832)

ACTIVE BEINGS

Even if you can only start out with one activity once in a while, give yourself credit for doing it. If you play regularly, count the times that you do play, not the days missed. Over the months and years, the gradual changes in your lifestyle will reward you with improved mental and physical health. You will feel, eat, and sleep better. In short, you will be a happier, more fulfilled person because of your new activity. Thank yourself for these new fun times in your life and love each moment.

YOUR ATHLETIC SELF

With the new societal attitude and acceptance that strength is beautiful, this shift in thinking is every woman's invitation to go play. The possibilities are everywhere and not just limited to what was considered acceptable for women in the past, such as dance, tennis, gymnastics, and figure skating.

Why not draw on your past experiences when you loved to cycle, jog, or swim? The door is open to you. What are you waiting for? Go outside and find the fun life offers to those who seek it.

> *Girls aren't less coordinated. Coordination has a lot to do with experience…*
> *and everyone has the ability to be coordinated.*
> —*Jamila Wideman (b.1975), 1997 Stanford basketball player, WNBA player for*
> *teams in Los Angeles; Cleveland, Ohio; and Portland, Oregon*

CREATIVE BEINGS

Scores of female musicians, writers, and artists have gone before to show the way for any hesitant creative soul—now all you have to do is follow. Let our distant sisters' brilliant art, music, and prose encourage you to engage in or expand your creative play.

To gain a better perspective on women in the arts, start your own journey based on curiosity. Explore their artistic worlds to learn techniques and tricks. Follow their courage, but rely on your own imagination. See your trek as an expression of yourself to release your creative muse to write, draw, paint, compose—to create.

- Mary Lou Williams (1910–1981), pianist, composer, and arranger known as the "first lady of the jazz keyboard," was the only major jazz artist who lived and played through all of its eras: the Spirituals, Ragtime, the Blues, the Kansas City Swing, Boogie-Woogie, and Bop or Modern, including religious and even the Avant-Garde.
- Georgia O'Keeffe (1887–1986) offered the world her bold flower paintings, which earned her the affectionate title of "a national treasure."
- Edith Wharton (1862–1937) was awarded the Pulitzer Prize for her book, *The Age of Innocence,* in 1920.
- Mexican painter Frida Kahlo (1907–1954), hailed as the twentieth century's quintessential autobiographical artist, suffered multiple injuries in a bus accident at the age of eighteen, yet continued to paint in spite of her many operations, lengthy hospital stays, and convalescence. Through pain and life-long disabilities, her indomitable will to create won.

YOUR ARTISTIC SELF

For creative play, choose your own medium—be it pastels, pottery, or photography. Your fun may be found in the kitchen creating unique tastes or in the sewing room exploring with color and fabric or needle and thread. Admit to yourself that, "I want to learn to paint with watercolors," or, "I want to write children's books," and either join a support-ive group or venture out on your own. Give in to your hidden passion and free your spir-it to do what it truly desires.

> *Every child is an artist.*
> *The problem is how to remain an artist when you grow up.*
> —*Pablo Picasso (1881–1973)*

Focus on now—stay in the moment—and be pleasantly surprised at what this time brings to your life. Give your passion time to grow and expand, time to climb to the next level, to become a greater part of you. Your journey for true creative expression will be its own reward.

> *May you live all the days of your life.*
> —*Jonathan Swift (1667–1745)*

BEING GOOD ENOUGH
Let me listen to me and not to them.
—*Gertrude Stein (1874–1946)*

What does it mean to be good enough? Are you preventing yourself from "doing" or "being" because you do not think that you are good enough?

Other people have expressed themselves in music, the arts, and sports because they believe they were good enough. Take their lead, follow their advice. There are scores of autobiographies and biographies to share the ideas and values that they believed in.

Go learn and apply these positive thoughts, actions, and words to your world. You do not have to shoot for stardom. Do it for yourself. Start feeling, acting, speaking, and thinking as if you are good enough. Make that list of what you need to get started and then dive in. Be sure to check off your accomplishments as you add this dimension to your life and prove to yourself that you are indeed, "good enough."

In a recent letter from my friend Joanne, she said, "I plan to shoot pool every day to get good at something—my new sport."

Go Joanne!

I couldn't get away from the fact that I was a girl playing hockey and not just a hockey player....I had to dress in the bathroom (rather than the locker room) and the girls watching and sometimes the parents would laugh at me as though I was doing something wrong...but I am glad I stuck with hockey, I'm glad I didn't listen to all those people.
—*Cammi Granato (b. 1971), 1998 Olympic Gold Medallist U.S. Hockey Team*

A Lady with Lyre
by Charles Edward Halle

CHAPTER TWO

The Truth about Play

WHY WE SHOULD

In our play, we reveal what kind of people we are.
—Ovid, Roman poet (43 B.C.–A.D. 17?)

Play is part of being human, yet it remains an elusive part of many women's lives. Studies have proven play is a major factor in the appropriate development of social, emotional, mental, and physical growth for children. But what happens when we stop playing as adults? Are we stunting our own growth? Why do humans play? Is it a requirement of survival like breathing, eating, and sleeping?

Play introduces the concept of "balance" in a busy life; it encourages women to seek solitude in nature and allocate time for daily laughs. Humor is needed to reaffirm our humanity and sanity. Laughter releases tension and stress, and builds rapport among those it touches. It is through our play that we are reintroduced to both once again.

In this time spent developing, challenging, and nurturing the authentic self, the promise of play—happiness— will be found.

The more passions and desires one has,
the more ways one has of being happy.
—Charlotte-Catherine de Gramont (1639–1678),
seventeenth-century Princess of Monaco

Play encourages interaction, risk-taking, and the use of imagination. Abstract thinking and creativity is explored, and social, language, and mental skills are mastered, as self-worth is strengthened. The value of dedication and practice is also learned. As such competencies are developed, these skills cross over to other aspects of life.

Based on these inherent benefits of play, recess should be reinstated for those over the age of ten. Until that day—why not decide to make play a frequent event in your life and add an hour or two of active play and creative expression to each week? It may seem like child's play at first, but once the magic starts, there will be no question that this is what your spirit needs.

Play is any activity that makes what was bothering you
"insignificant."
—Penny Hamilton, Steamboat Springs, Colorado

Genuine play occurs when you lose sight of yourself and your life for the moment. You are totally immersed in whatever physical or creative activity with no awareness of the passing of time. You are truly awake and alive. For some people, play may be more physical. For others, it is a creative outlet for expression. However, both types of play can satisfy our basic need for curiosity, exploration, and fun.

Play is any activity that lets me let go of my adulthood and frees me of stress. This could include, for me, playing board games or running in the autumn leaves.
—Debbie Curd, Chicago, Illinois

In the choice for a long and healthy life, playing is not just an option, but also a natural element of each day. Moving the body is as crucial as eating and sleeping. It is a proven fact that increased physical activity—a hike, jog, or a round of tennis—results in increased "smarts."

According to medical studies by the University of Michigan, physical exercise can improve your mental and physical health.

Physical activity is an essential part of long-term health. As play is added to your days, you will begin to see that the amount of time spent playing is in direct correlation with the amount of energy you have. Your newfound interest will also keep mood swings in check, help manage stress, and build a stronger immune system.

According to the American Heart Association, increased levels of activity
have proven to reduce coronary heart disease, hypertension, non-insulin-dependent
Type 2 diabetes, colon cancer, depression, and anxiety.

A HEALTHY BODY
If we don't take good care of our bodies, where will we live?
—*Anonymous*

Play is so good for our bodies. No matter your size, shape, weight, or height, adding play to your life will improve your self-image. When we become too busy to play, we fall prey to diet fads or bad habits like smoking. Playing hard and eating well will do wonders not only for your temperament, but for your body, too.

As of December 2001, the Centers for Disease Control and Prevention announced
findings that 61 percent of U.S. adults are overweight.

America is obsessed with weight, yet we are a nation of overweight people. Fast food restaurants taunt twenty-four hours a day with appetizing, four-color images of the four food groups: burgers, french fries, soda, and dessert. It is no wonder the average U.S. child grows up not knowing what is healthy food. There is no safe haven unless you shop at a health food store or the perimeter of a grocery chain where the fresh produce, meats, breads, and dairy are housed. Ironically, that is where the four food groups are kept.

2002—McDonald's is the largest global foodservice retailer, with more than thirty thousand restaurants in 121 countries.

In the mail, magazines, and newspapers or on the radio and television, prolific diet ads tell women to fix their bodies with their constant message: "Everyone can lose weight."

The National Eating Disorder Association estimates that 40 to 50 percent of women in America are trying to lose weight at any point in time and spend more than $40 billion dollars annually on diet programs and related products. This amount is roughly equivalent to what the U.S. government spends on education each year.

These weight-loss promises set up many people for failure prior to even starting. Those who do attempt and fall short are then convinced that there is something wrong with them.

The American Lung Association reports that nearly twenty-two million women smoke, and most claim that the number one reason they do so is to control their weight. In 1987, lung cancer surpassed breast cancer as the leading cause of death among U.S. women.

No one looks like the models in the countless fashion magazines and direct mail catalogs—not even the women photographed. They are air-brushed to perfection.

According to a recent survey by Girls Incorporated, more than 70 percent of women feel depressed after spending only three minutes with a fashion magazine.

Try this: Hold up any photo of a woman found in a magazine ad or direct mail catalog. Turn it upside-down and look at the so-called "natural" curves of this model. Is she real?

Sometimes it is hard to tell. There is a very strong chance that this model—who is posing as an adult—is indeed still in her teens, suffers from an eating disorder, has a computer-altered body, or all of the above.

According to the American College of Obstetricians and Gynecologists, about one-third of the roughly fifteen million people who abuse alcohol in the United States are women.

In her book *The Beauty Myth* author Naomi Wolf detailed how big business keeps women buying. Their messages today hit where it hurts—at face value. The new marketing mantra everywhere is: "Stay beautiful and young forever."

The American Society for Aesthetic Plastic Surgery reported a 304 percent increase in procedures from 1997 to 2001. Nearly 8.5 million cosmetic surgical and non-surgical (Botox) procedures were performed in 2001 alone.

The biggest tragedy facing women today is not this reliance on diets, cigarettes, alcohol, or surgery, but the missing awareness of the mind-body connection. This is why play, through both active and creative expression, is so important. Play is meant to draw us closer to our own reflection, to see what is really inside our complicated yet beautiful selves. The desire to move, the desire to create, is and should be a required element of every woman's day. It is the truth behind what makes us who we are.

FOR BALANCE

A vigorous walk will do more good for an unhappy, but otherwise healthy adult than all the medicine and psychology in the world.
—*Dr. Paul Dudley White (1886–1973), Founder of the American Heart Association*

With advertising messages so loud and prominent, we can no longer hear our internal hunger cues. Many times our thirst is mistaken for hunger. We may think it is food that our stomachs want when it is actually our bodies crying out for rest, attention, play, or love.

Stop dieting and start living today. Release yourself from your inner voice that keeps the promise alive: "Once I am a certain pant size or hit the magical number on the scale, my life will be great."

Eat for your health and love your body for what it can do for you right now. Seek balance in your physical activity, creative expression, food consumption, rest, and work. Eat birthday cake and then go for a walk with the party afterwards. Balance is the key—it always has been and always will be. With gentle encouragement, begin to unveil the woman that you were meant to be. Speak softly but firmly, and listen. You are wiser than you allow yourself to be.

> *Liken yourself to a beautiful original part of creation—*
> *a true work of art.*
> *Then each day ask yourself how you are living: either*
> *in ways that show gratitude for this beauty or*
> *in ways that indicate how you are defacing it.*
> —Robert J. Wicks (b. 1946)

INNER BEAUTY

Beauty is not in the face; beauty is a light in the heart.
—Kahlil Gibran (1883–1931)

There is an easy solution to end the love/hate relationship that so many women have with food and their bodies.

Be yourself. Be your complete and authentic self—not what you think others want you to be or what society pressures women to be. Express yourself with your body and your mind by being you, the person who you are supposed to be. Use your time, energy, and money, not on dieting, but on passionate living achieved by body-moving activities and mind-engaging interests.

Beauty…is something felt, a glow, or communicated sense of fineness. What ails us is that our sense of beauty is so bruised and blunted, we miss all the best.
—D.H. Lawrence (1885–1930)

When a person builds herself from the inside out, she shines bright with hope, promise, and life. Nothing can shake her world; she is anchored by being herself. When you meet a woman who has granted herself approval, acceptance, and love, she no longer has a dieting or weight problem. She has found herself.

Self-love is the only weight-loss aid that really works in the long run.
—Jenny Craig (b.1932)

YOUR LOYAL COMPANION

As we go through many changes in our lives, play gives us the ability to react and cope. At the age of twenty, after my mother died unexpectedly, I needed something to ground me. I returned to my loyal companion from my childhood, my bike.

Cycling is a sport easy on the body and can be done until you are as old as the *Tour de France*. Riding a bike is like the road of life; sometimes it is difficult with steep grades and bumpy terrain. Other times, it seems as if the propelling tail winds and endless flat stretches will carry you forever.

In 2003, the twenty-one–day, 2,000+ mile bicycle race Tour de France celebrated its one-hundredth birthday. Today, there is also a Tour de France bike race held for women each August.

Whether we play in clay, flour, our gardens, or take to the paths on our feet, roller blades, or a horse—the experience and skill stays with us. Pick up a new sport or a hobby and make it part of you. Keep an element of play in your life.

> *I've always felt running is a form of meditation. Running enables us to stop our lives, to go out and find a safe place for ourselves.*
> —*Nina Kuscsik (b. 1939), first woman to run in the New York City Marathon, and two-time winner and the first female winner of the Boston Marathon*

Why We Should Play

On your busy days, or when motivation is lacking, remind yourself why you want to play and create a list of reasons and benefits gained from partaking in your new healthy habit. Post this list (or your own) somewhere where it will keep you playing well and often.

Reasons to Play

Be More Energetic.

Develop a Positive Attitude.

Add a New Accomplishment to Life.

Acquire a Sense of Peace.

Regulate Mood Swings.

Enhance Self-Esteem.

Boost Self-Confidence.

Develop Discipline.

Be Committed.

Have Fun and Smile More!

Carry laughter with you wherever you go.
—*Hugh Sidney (b. 1927)*

The Favourite
by John William Godward

CHAPTER THREE

Creating Time for Play

NEEDS VS. DESIRES

Play is letting your mind be free of work.
—*Keri Seals, Denver, Colorado.*

With all the responsibilities in our days, it is sometimes difficult to make the time to go play, but it can be done.

Repetitive household tasks—dishes, laundry, and cleaning—will try to get you to stay inside. Do not listen. Close your eyes to the mess and go. Once outside, shake off that feeling of responsibility for the moment and feel your spirit soar. After your play session, your step will be lighter, your heart happier, and you will have more energy to tackle whatever needs to be done. Trust me on this matter of guilt. I have fought this battle so many times, I have lost count but not sight of what is important—my health and sanity.

I am always amazed how after I make the decision to create the time to do what I want to do, the deleted items from my daily list become insignificant—or at least can wait until tomorrow.

How to Find More Hours

1. Quit a committee that drains you.
2. Eliminate an obligation.
3. Delegate a responsibility.
4. Change your mind.
5. Cancel.
6. Say "no."

Guilt is a rope that wears thin.
—*Ayn Rand (1905–1982)*

FUN EVERY DAY

What does "fun" mean to you? Originally, the word meant "a trick, a hoax, or to cheat," and was probably derived from the Middle Age word *fon* or *fonne*, which is a foolish person. Today, the word can be used as an adjective or a noun. Either way, this word needs to be part of our busy days. Be on the lookout for any occasion, official or from your imagination, to invite fun, laughter, and play into your hours.

The closest date that can be identified as the start of April Fool's Day, also called All Fool's Day, is 1582 in France. Originally, the first day of the new year was April 1, but this changed once Pope Gregory introduced the new calendar for the Christian world, moving the date earlier to January 1. This news did not reach some until years later and those obstinate

about the change who did not conform were called fools by the general populace.
This harassment evolved over time into a tradition of pranks, jokes, and gags.

According to Chase's Calendar of Events, September 3 is Play Day.

Remember the good old whoopee cushion? This inexpensive and still available gag may be just what your household needs to get the laughs started.

Looking foolish does the spirit good.
—John Updike (b. 1932)

Assign yourself the role of stand-up comic. Pull a few joke books from the library and be the one your friends and family can count on for a good joke. (Even if you mess up the punch line as I do, your act of telling a joke will still be funny.)

Chase's Calendar of Events lists January 25 as Fun at Work Day.

When we enjoy our work, we are more productive. Make work a laughing matter—at least at the start of each weekday. Buy a joke calendar and share with your officemates. Make a conscious effort to add more levity into each and every day. Your time can be reading the Sunday comics, five minutes with a joke book, or ninety minutes watching a comedy video. And do not wait until April Fool's Day to pull a practical joke—any day can be prime for such playfulness. Decide to laugh a lot today and make someone else laugh, too.

Dreams Do Come True

My grandfather once said to me, "First, you have your health and time, but no money. Then you have your health and money, but no time. And at the end of your life, you have time and money, but no health."

> *The great dividing line between success and failure can be*
> *expressed in five words: "I did not have time."*
> —*Anonymous*

Listen to the voice inside of you that is growing louder, too loud to be ignored. Trust your inner voice and decide to play today. The results will definitely be worth your effort. Decide to tackle your passion on a part-time basis and follow your dream no matter how long it might take to reach. This action of beginning will make life so much sweeter and each moment that you spend there, precious.

> *To thine own self be true...*
> —*William Shakespeare (1564–1616), Hamlet, Act I, Scene iii, Line 78*

Put your dream to paper; once captured in words, it becomes alive. There is hope and power to its achievement. Tuck your handwritten note in your lingerie drawer. Now, every day when you dress, you will see your words, the validation that you are making time for more fun, laughs, and smiles in your hours. By moving toward your dreams, you will see the impact that play can make on your life.

SMALL TEACHERS AND CREATURES

Learn from the masters and inventors of play: children. These little wonders are always on a journey of fun, seeking pleasure. Watch a puppy or kitten play. It is a spontaneous act, yet the most natural movement in the world. We could learn much from the antics of these small creatures. The company of animals is good for us, too, and can enhance our good health and well-being.

All I need to know I learned from my cat.
—*Suzy Becker (b.1962)*

Pet lovers have always known this to be true. Twenty-five years ago, the first study of this human-companion bond proved that heart attack patients who had a pet had a faster recovery and lived longer. Now, in almost every city across America, animal-assisted psychotherapy programs are in existence, bringing pets to hospitals, nursing homes, and other rehabilitation facilities for regular healing visits. Four-legged creatures—gerbils, rabbits, puppies, kittens, and ponies—are a great comfort.

A dog wags its tail with its heart.
—Martin Buxbaum (1912–1991)

To help the neurologically impaired who cannot walk, an equestrian therapy, called hippotherapy, was developed. Under the supervision of licensed therapists, the individual sits on a horse, holds the reins, and benefits from the horse's gait as it walks. Their bodies must adjust to the motion of the animal, which stimulates the muscle neurons firing similarly to when a person is walking.

Floyd perks me up. Dogs never have a bad run. They're not judgmental.
I learned from Floyd that even if a run wasn't great, we still got it in. We ran.
—Regina Jacobs (b. 1963), four-time Olympian

Pets are great reminders to get us to play regularly. They never let a day slip by without playing—we should not either. Let Felix or Fido show you how to play again. Fill a box, crate, or bucket with various sizes of balls, a knotted rope, a Frisbee, or stuffed animals made for pets, and you will be guaranteed hours of abundant amusement.

When you play with your pet, your dog drops the guilt trip.
—*Chris Hermann, Basking Ridge, New Jersey*

If your household is without a fluffy companion, why not take the route of being a part-time owner? You can enjoy all the fun of playing with a small creature without any of the hassles or messes, rather similar to being an aunt. If a next-door neighbor works all day, offer to pet-sit. You set the hours and the days. Or maybe you can simply volunteer for one of the dog's daily walks or to check on the kittens in the afternoon.

Another alternative to owning a pet is to be a regular at the local animal shelter. The staff will welcome your offers to walk the dogs and play with the kittens. If you were determined before to stay pet-free, you may find yourself changing your mind about having a pet, especially after a small, fluffy creature looks into your eyes and crawls into your lap. The wag of a tail or the contented purring of a kitten is an instant "pick me up" remedy.

MINUTES COUNT

Lack of willpower has caused more failure than lack of intelligence or ability.
—*Flower A. Newhouse (1909–1994)*

My writer friend, Elizabeth, is a working mother, so her time to write is precious. She has implemented a fifteen-minute writing strategy and is thrilled that she can squeeze her passion into every day. By allocating time in small blocks, she has set goals that are achievable and rewarding.

Encourage your creative self to explore the endless possibilities for expression. Attend a local art show, appreciate the work that goes into each piece, and start working on your submission. If you want to be a writer, read about how to develop believable characters or an effective plot, or practice organizing your thoughts and opinions in letters to the editor. Stephen King once said, "If you write a page a day, you will have a book a year."

Freedom Found

I'm not going to vacuum 'til Sears makes one you can ride.
—Roseanne Barr (b.1953)

Freedom to experiment with what the spirit truly seeks will deliver positive returns four-fold to you: emotionally, physically, mentally, and spiritually. You will be ready for anything from this strong base. You are not being selfish. This time spent in unadulterated bliss will do your spirit a world of good. Your family and career will also benefit from your brand new expression.

Acknowledge to yourself and those close to you that this change is not going to be a weekend fling, but a new lifestyle change that will do you and everyone around you good. Talk to your significant other and your family to express how important this change is to you.

Approach your boss about your passion, and request to rework the hours in one day a week or a couple of days a month. Bike to work, walk to work, take a class at night. Ask to start a company bowling, skiing, softball, golf, tennis, or volleyball team in the name of employee morale, teamwork, and fun. Explain how this new endeavor will make you and others better employees—with this extra energy, your productivity will soar. Set up a trial run to prove to your employer that play can and will pay.

2002—The League of American Bicyclists marked its forty-sixth consecutive year of promoting its annual Bike to Work Week from May 13–17 and Bike to Work Day on Friday, May 17. This May, do something good for the environment (and for yourself) and join the thousands who will bike to work, or sponsor this event at your office.

Play at the Office or While Traveling

- *Make an appointment for play—before work, at lunch, or after work—and do not cancel.*
- *Instead of taking another coffee break, walk around the office building.*
- *Being outdoors will energize both your body and mind.*
- *If you travel for business, book a hotel with a gym and/or pool and use them.*

SIMPLIFY
At the worst, a house unkempt cannot be so distressing as a life unlived.
—Rose Macaulay (1881–1958)

In the weeks ahead, simplify all aspects of your life. Adopt abbreviated household cleaning, personal self-care, and cooking routines. Add one change at a time to make sure the new idea sticks and works for you.

Play is time to myself to do the things I enjoy.
—Dottie Para, Teaneck, New Jersey

Laundry Time-Savers
Do all of the laundry in one day.
Announce that "TV time" is "folding-the-laundry-time."
Use bath towels for three days.
Share dry cleaning drops and pick-ups with a neighbor.
Teach your family members how to do their own laundry.

Discuss your plans to play with your roommates, significant other, children, or others, and let them know you need and want their help. Expand your time in each day by sharing or delegating chores.

"Mom" is not another word for "maid," so give the troops their own duties to make them a contributing member of the family—no matter what age. You will be teaching them, and yourself, new life skills.

Clean the house in record time. Instead of reaching for a cup of joe, slip Jane Ira Bloom's latest release into the CD player. Arabesque Jazz has all of the spirit and spontaneity of a live jazz concert, guaranteed to get your cleaning done faster with such a tempo.

Household Time-Savers

Set a Time Limit. *For repetitive household tasks, set a timer to clean each room.*

Enlist Help. *Play energetic music and work together to get the chores done faster.*

Teach the Kids. *Let them listen to their headsets while vacuuming.*

Multi-Task: *Use a cordless phone with headset to return calls and make appointments while dusting and washing the windows.*

Favorite Color: *Use the same color towels throughout the house. White can always look great with a little bleach.*

Every Time: *Put a squeegee in the shower stall and clean the doors after every shower.*

Squeaky Clean: *Keep a roll of paper towels in the bathrooms to wipe down the counters whenever needed.*

Whenever Necessary: *Transfer window cleaner to a smaller spray bottle and keep the bathroom mirror clean while brushing your teeth.*

Use Your Feet. *Buy a pair of floor-cleaning slippers and skate around your wooden and tile floors for a quick spot cleaning.*

Cleaning your house while your kids are still growing is like
shoveling the walk before it stops snowing.
—Phyllis Diller (b. 1917)

Remember, schedules can be rearranged, altered, or changed. Pull out a calendar and work together on achieving this promise of play. List and discuss all of the household chores to learn if there are one or two that someone actually does not mind doing and then sign them up.

If all else fails, extend the invitation to have them to join you in your new fun, but only after the dishes are done as a collective effort.

Meal Time-Savers

- Prep single-serving snacks including veggies and fruit for lunches.
- The night before, bake or buy fruit muffins for breakfast so you can take this time in the morning to play.
- Let the Crock-Pot cook dinner regularly.
- Double a cookie or dinner recipe and freeze half for next week.
- Use paper plates once a week to free up time after dinner.
- Order out once a week.
- Save any leftovers for tomorrow's lunch.
- Buy a prepared grocery store dinner.
- Take turns cooking.

Work with your partner and family to block any obstacles in your life that keep play out of your day. Discuss the matter with them—write a letter or send an email if you must—telling them why you believe play is important and why you must do it.

Advantages to Playing at Home

It is convenient and available any of the twenty-four hours in a day.
Be comfortable—wear anything and forget about your hair.
Set a good example for everyone in the household.

CHANGE YOUR CLOTHES

By implementing a gradual change in clothing to be more comfortable and casual, you can still be professional when necessary and now always ready for fun and play. If you love to walk, toss a pair of sneakers in the trunk of your car. Go walk at lunch. Do not worry if your walking shoes do not match your suit. Worry if your body does not get the daily walk it desires.

If high heels were so wonderful, men would still be wearing them.
—*Sue Grafton (b.1940)*

Personal Care Tips

Basic Colors: *Reduce your wardrobe to a few basic colors. Pick the hues and tones that look best with your skin and hair color. Mix and match tops and bottoms for endless stylish outfits. (Bonus Tip: Monochromatic clothing has a slimming effect.)*

Flattery: *Get a haircut that flatters your face and your lifestyle to cut the time spent in the bathroom in half.*

Simple Beauty: *Clean out your makeup drawer, bag, or cabinet——get one good concealer, mascara, lipstick, and eye shadow. Toss the rest, or easier yet, do not wear makeup at all. Use a good cleanser, moisturizer, and sunscreen, and get out the door faster to play.*

I base most of my fashion tastes on what doesn't itch.
—Gilda Radner (1946–1989)

Carpe diem (Latin for "Seize the day")

Discover your best time for play. For a few weeks, track whether your body responds better in the morning or later in the day. Once you have tested various times, you can determine an ideal schedule.

Some weeks, a plan must be in place in order to find the time to play. Write the designated time on your calendar. Put a note on the kitchen counter to remind you of your priorities today when you awake. Pack for play. Put your gym bag, art kit, or knitting box in the car, by the front door—wherever you will see it to remind you to go play. The night before, lay out your sweats for an early morning run. Sometimes, just savoring the upcoming bout of play is enough to motivate us through what we need to do.

Other weeks just drop everything and go. No plans—just total spontaneity. Whatever you are doing can (usually) wait. Give it a try. You will be amazed at the amount of energy that you will have when you return.

This week make that "reservation for one" at your favorite place for play. Consider this money and time well spent, and call it "preventive health insurance," which is better than its alternative—paying for doctor visits, prescription medicine, and spending time in the hospital.

As you participate, a new respect and appreciation for your body will take root and grow. You will see that a strong body and mind are to be celebrated. Make a commitment to play, make it an integral part of your life.

> *It's never too late in fiction or life to revise.*
> —*Nancy Thayer (b. 1943)*

A Boating Party
by John Singer Sargent

CHAPTER FOUR

Motivational Tips

BRIBES, CHARMS, AND TRICKS

Yesterday is but a dream, and tomorrow is only a vision,
but today well lived makes every yesterday a dream
of happiness and every tomorrow a vision of hope.
—*Unknown*

Fitness and women's magazines as well as the health section of most newspapers are filled with well-intended motivational tips to help us begin an exercise program. Clipped, highlighted, and filed away, these words of advice never seem to move us to do more than just that. We join a gym and then let the membership card stay at home, with us.

The latest board games, recently released books, and brand new tools and toys arrive home and sit in the cabinet for years untouched. Craft, hobby, and art ideas also collect in the "want to do" pile, but somehow the hours escape us, and our intention of "doing" waits again for tomorrow. Change takes time. Finding the motivation to "go play" can be a difficult concept for many.

My advice is to employ

seductive bribes and good luck charms, or trick the mind to get yourself to go play. Any way you approach motivation, you cannot lose. My motto is, "Whatever works."

Go confidently in the direction of your dreams! Live the life you've imagined.
—*Henry David Thoreau (1817–1862)*

SEDUCTIVE BRIBES
I never practice, I only play.
—*Wanda Landowska (1877–1959)*

Rely on a bribe—such as the promise of a new item of clothing, an extra treat, or something you've had your eye on for a while—whenever your motivation is lacking or interest is waning. This compelling purchase can help spark renewed energy into an old passion or erase your hesitancy to venture into new territory. Nine times out of ten, bribes work.

AFFIRMATIONS
Men still buy toys and tools as grownups—golf clubs, mountain bikes, fishing tackle, or a Swiss army pocket knife—why shouldn't women?

Go shopping for a new toy or tool and watch the level of your excitement accelerate.

My creative friend, Linda, bought herself a color copier for her art studio and now makes beautiful decoupage mini-books, boxes, and greeting cards.

PLAY FIRST

By allowing the option to reorganize the day and priorities, you can bribe yourself to do what you have to do in order to do what you want to do—or vice versa. Put your painting time first. Morning light is better anyhow. Schedule your run early so that you can bank on this energy later in the day. You will be glad you did.

BOOK IT

The commitment to others makes play happen regularly, too. By setting up a schedule with others or booking your time with an objective in mind, getting out the door will be much easier. The prospect of seeing your friends will reward you for the effort of getting ready, and happiness has a way of making events repeat.

ERASE BOREDOM

Rotate the good times. This strategy works whether you are playing in paints or playing golf. For example, on some days, go solo for your run or discovery of a new author at the local bookstore. On other days, join the group to paint by the river's edge or hike a distant peak. Reserve extra time in the days of the week that start with the letter "T" or "S." Start each month knowing that by the month's end, you will be tallying the time, miles, or number of crafts created—just for fun. But you'll see, as your tally increases, that you'll find yourself more and more motivated. Create a prize for yourself when you've reached your goal. And a prize at halfway can work wonders, too.

CHANGE IS GOOD

Once a week, give your body and mind a rest from your main play activity and substitute a new sport or activity to develop other skills. If you kickbox for fun, jump in the pool instead. Pull out the *mancala* board instead of playing chess again. Reward your consistency with your chosen activity by offering yourself something new from time to time. By mixing up your play options, when you do return to your true love, it will be fresh and new again.

BECOME A PRO

Happiness lies in the joy of achievement and the thrill of creative effort.
—*Franklin D. Roosevelt (1882–1945)*

I made the mistake of getting in a sailboat with a friend who had only read about the sport. As we tacked farther and farther from shore, I realized the value of knowing technique and knowing it well.

To step up your current level of skill, sign up for a class. A personal trainer or private instructor can help, too, whether you are learning how to maneuver a snowboard through the bumps, lift weights, or master the scales on the piano. The prospect of gaining additional knowledge and mastery can make your play more enjoyable and keep you going when your enthusiasm flags.

GOOD LUCK CHARMS

What an immense power over life is the power of possessing distinct aims.
The voice, the dress, the look, the very motions of a person, define and
alter when he or she begins to live for a reason.
—*Elizabeth Stuart Phelps (1844–1911)*

Following a dream has been a source of inspiration and education for many scientists, writers, artists, and inventors who embarked on their own personal voyage of discovery. Let them motivate you to new heights in your active and creative play.

Capture or commemorate all of your achievements to encourage yourself to reach for other goals. You can do this with writings, souvenirs, or any other tangible token of a triumph. (What do you think trophies are for?) I call them my good luck charms because whenever I see them or hold them in my hands, good things happen.

Save all of your dreams. They are your hope for the future.

WALL OF INSPIRATION

Why does the eye see a thing more clearly in
dreams than the imagination when awake?
—*Leonardo da Vinci (1452–1519)*

In my office, I have dedicated an entire wall to sources of inspiration: my daughter, my husband, my health (a picture of my husband and me mountain biking), a copy of the advance check from my first book, and the titles of books that I plan to write.

I also have posted brilliant quotes, cartoons, jokes, slips from fortune cookies, greeting cards sent by friends, family, readers, and fabulous art by old-world masters, by my daughter, and even my own sketches and watercolor paintings. Yes, it is a mess, but a happy mess. One glance at my "inspiration wall" and I cannot help but be motivated. This instant blast of appreciation for all that is good in my world encourages me to keep playing and discovering more fun.

The day the Lord created hope was probably the same day he created Spring.
—*Anonymous*

DREAM JOURNALS

On days when my creativity tank is running on low, I page through my dream journal. It is a clunky, three-ring binder filled with pages that can hold photos, but I chose to put pictures of my dreams instead.

Inside are pictures of beautiful gardens that I aspire to create one day, travel destinations such as Machu Picchu and the Swiss Alps, and the color I will soon paint my bathroom. Included are also smaller, more attainable dreams: a picture and recipe of a refreshing beverage for the lazy afternoon when I want to treat my husband and myself, a simple flower arrangement idea using recycled colored bottles and wild-flowers.

I find other ideas in my junk mail. Direct mail catalogs show me new ways to layer colors and mix styles. Labels from imported bottles and packages provide the inspiration to create a greeting card or a decoupage lampshade with foreign words and designs.

> *All inspirations start as frail as a redwood seed,*
> *yet can grow to be the mightiest of trees.*
> —*Anonymous*

POSTCARDS

I love to get "real" mail: letters, cards, and postcards. To make sure my mailbox is full of the good wishes, I send myself postcards whenever I am away on a venture. I do this for two reasons: these postcards always remind me of how much fun I had, and the pictures are much better than what I can take.

I started this habit about ten years ago and am still surprised at how a postcard from the Kern River can bring up the entire rafting trip in my mind. Try this yourself, or designate one friend as your pen pal and send each other notes, letters, clippings, recipes, and, yes, postcards.

ADVENTURE ALBUMS

To accomplish great things, we must not only act,
but also dream, not only plan, but also believe.
—Anatole France (1844–1924)

The essential oil of juniper (juniperus communis) is an excellent stimulator.
In a ceramic amphora filled with water, place a few drops to motivate you, or add
seven drops to your morning bath to ready your body for your active play session.

Memory is powerful medicine. With a few postcards, photos, the bed-and-breakfast brochure, the campsite receipt, matchbook covers from restaurants, the ticket stubs, or the map from a great trip, you can put together a good luck charm to get you planning your next adventure. Bottle that feeling of fun and revisit your adventure album often to remember the strong self that is still inside of you.

PLAY JOURNALS

I love my bicycle!
—Kathy Diemer, Chicago, Illinois

Keep a play journal—any blank book to record the miles, list books to read, or capture your sessions of "free writing." Write down the start dates of your dreams, and then go off in search of fulfillment. The best part of this charm is that bragging is permitted.

Get an odometer for your bike or a pedometer for your runs, hikes, or walks. Count the laps you swim, the yoga classes attended this month, or the number of times you get to the tennis or basketball courts. Along your journey, record how you felt, any successes or setbacks encountered. Draw five stars if you had an excellent time or a sad face if you did not feel well on this particular day. When you achieve your dream, record this wondrous sensation and celebrate the milestone.

Whenever you lose interest or motivation, reread your play journal to get back on track. From twenty years of bike riding, I have filled many cycling logs and resort to reading the pages on lazy days to get me on the road or trail again.

As you review your journal—a week, month, or years later—you will relive many of the play sessions and feel a sense of pride. You did it. You made the time for fun. You now possess the confidence gained from such accomplishments and know the difference that carrying muscle and new knowledge can make. Return to these pages regularly to remember the person who you were before the challenge and acknowledge who you have become. Also, rely on these memories to propel you to try something new and equally daring as you once thought these accomplishments to be.

Trick the Mind

The average number of steps that we take in a day is estimated to be about five thousand. By doubling this amount of steps, you can add the equivalent of a thirty-minute workout of moderate activity to your day. Use a pedometer to keep count.

Welcome motion into your life and use your body as intended. All activity counts. Any type of movement equates to calories expended and provides a reserve of energy to tap later. Try a few of these tricks to stimulate your body, which will in turn wake up your mind.

Tricks around the House

Start each morning with three minutes of gentle stretches in bed.

Walk the dog (or yourself) twice a day.

Dance with the kids or yourself.

Run in the house.

Leap over piles in the hall.

Use a treadmill or exercise bike, or do yoga or other stretches, while watching TV.

Walk during your lunch break today.

Run around the playground with your children instead of watching from the bench.

Grab a backpack, put on comfortable shoes, and walk to do your errands.

Office Tricks

A new genre of jazz, called acid jazz, is a good motivator.

Try Karl Denson's Dance Lesson #2 *for a new twist on problem-solving at the office.*

Open-plan work areas and cubicles are often stuffy and not conducive to clear thinking. Useful essential oils for the office include bergamot (*citrus bergamia*) which is refreshing and uplifting; melissa (*melissa officinalis*) with its familiar lemon aroma is said to remove tension yet lift the spirit; rosemary (*rosmarinus officinalis*), a great aid for concentration; or basil (*ocimum basilicum*) to stimulate a tired brain.

Indian tea or chai (the Hindi word for tea) is also a wonderful stimulant for after lunch. You can make your own *massala*, mixture of spices, and bring it to work in a thermos.

Indian Tea

1½ cups of water
⅛ teaspoon of cardamom
⅛ teaspoon of ginger
8 whole cloves
A pinch of black pepper
⅛ teaspoon of nutmeg
⅛ teaspoon of allspice

One-inch stick of vanilla bean
(or ¼ teaspoon of liquid)
One stick of cinnamon
(or ¼ teaspoon of powder)
⅔ cup of soy milk (or regular milk)
3 teaspoons black tea
(loose leaves preferably, or two tea bags)
Raw sugar cubes

Add water and spices to saucepan; simmer for eight minutes. Add milk; bring to simmer again, but not a boil. Add tea leaves and cover, turning off the heat. After two minutes, strain the beverage and serve with sugar to preference. Depending on the weather outside or your temperament of the day, Indian tea can be served hot or over ice.

Tricks at the Office

Park in the furthest spot and enjoy the short stroll.

Use the stairs instead of the elevator.

Use the restroom farthest from your area.

Stand when on the phone instead of sitting.

Visit coworkers on the next floor rather than emailing them.

Take your coffee break "to go" and walk outside for twenty minutes.

If waiting for the subway, train, or bus, pace or simply walk instead.

Energy Tip

Conquer late afternoon fatigue and the urge to eat junk food with deep breathing for five minutes with your shoes off, feet up, and eyes closed.

No Pressure

The greatest thing in this world is not so much where we are, but in what direction we are moving.

—*Oliver Wendell Holmes Jr. (1841–1935)*

I once had a yoga instructor in southern California, Carolyn, who always shared a vital message during every class: "Wherever you are, is exactly where you are supposed to be."

I wholeheartedly agree. Do not compare yourself to anyone. There is no competition. Do not judge yourself by others' standards. You are a unique individual. This is what makes the world a wonderful, dynamic, and interesting place to live. Play at your own pace.

Go Slowly

Many beginners, or those who have taken a long break from playing, have a tendency to go at it too fast and with too much intensity and simply burn out. Get started or return to your play—slowly. There are many more days in the year.

Energy Tip

For snack time, regularly treat yourself to a cup of herbal tea or a piece of fresh fruit to keep your energy level high for your afternoon session of play.

Mid-Year Resolutions

Set yourself up for success—make your resolutions in any month that works for you. Start your new year with any of the twelve months, and make the next 365 days the year that you will begin to sew, paint, write lyrics, or learn how to make stained glass windows. Do not let the fact that it isn't January stop you from achieving your dreams.

INSPIRATIONAL OTHERS

The wisest mind has something yet to learn.
—George Santayana (1863–1952)

Need help jumping back into a new sport or hobby? Learning can spark your ambition to play or create again. Employ the assistance of an instructor, coach, mentor, college professor, or a good friend avid about your potential interest. Ask your fitness club for recommendations of a personal trainer. Find someone who you feel will be supportive and will encourage you to become your best. Sometimes, all we need is a hint of inspiration from others to motivate ourselves.

A teacher affects eternity.
—Henry B. Adams (1838–1918)

Yes, you can return to your beloved team sport as an adult, just call the parks and recreational office to see what teams are now forming.

Yes, you can learn or return to playing the flute or piano.

Yes, you can dance: ballet, tap, ballroom, or hip hop. Ask around to find out who is giving private lessons or if there is an adult class starting.

Yes—just go.

Teachers open the door, but you must enter by yourself.
—Chinese proverb

POSITIVE THOUGHTS

Tell yourself that you are good at skiing, painting, singing—whatever you are attempting. The more you say these positive words to yourself, the more you will believe and become. Half the battle to becoming successful is overcoming attitudes and opinions, both our own and of those who set the narrow constraints of what should be.

Do a mental check of those who are around you regularly. If they are effervescent with energy and a positive outlook, stay close. For all the others, step away from their negative energy and comments. By surrounding yourself with good people, their energy, and encouraging words, you have set the stage for greatness.

ACCOUNTABILITY

Tell someone, anyone, about your new passion. Accountability will make you do things you originally did not think you could do. Once you commit your new sport or hobby to the spoken word, you are halfway there. There is power in the spoken statement. It says, "I believe in myself and I am going to do this."

There are no obstacles, only challenges.
—*Lord Louis Mountbatten (1900–1979)*

When I quit my day job to write full-time, I told everyone I was writing a book. Some writers believe if you tell anyone what you are doing, your creativity will be

*Play is when your mind,
body, and spirit are all laughing
and tickled to be doing
what you are doing.*
——*Miranda Rivera,
Montrose, Colorado*

threatened. I find the opposite is true. By telling others, writers and non-writers, you establish the anticipation of a finished product. For most creative types, finishing is a problem. It is simple to start the creative process, but difficult to complete.

Make a list and be sure to include the line item "Go Play" every day. If you cannot trust yourself to get out the door, book time with a friend so you are committed.

Inspire your creative self. Start an art portfolio, save your sketchbooks and journals, or transform your entire home into your own personal art gallery. When you find yourself questioning why you ever signed up for ceramics or are stalled for new ideas, look back through your art collection. Let your work speak for itself and for you. Examine how this woman has grown from the experience, and be moved to keep reaching for more time to explore and create.

TENNIS PLAYERS
BY HORACE HENRY CAUTY

CHAPTER FIVE

Active Play

GO OUTSIDE!

I cringe when I still hear an adult tell a young girl that she should not play sports because it is not attractive or put her down in another way. I wonder how many adult women today would still be playing if a parent, teacher, neighbor, or relative had not said anything but positive words. I wonder if this present surge of women athletes would have crested sooner and with a greater force.
—Julie Foudy (b. 1971), soccer, center mid-fielder, co-captain, 1996 Olympic Gold, four-time All-American player

We are not all born Olympians. In fact, only a few dozen of the female babies born today will ever wear gold medals around their necks. Most women will never be on a professional team, but does that mean we should not play?

In high school I was lousy in every sport. I hated P.E. But I joined the track team and fell in love with running. This helped me find myself.
—Jacqueline Hansen (b.1948), marathoner (the first woman to run under
2:40) twelve marathon wins, including Boston and Honolulu

The saddest thing in the world is wasted talent; all women have an innate ability for sports. It is simply the question of who plays and who does not. In some individuals such as professional athletes, this proficiency is very fine-tuned. In others, this raw ability has yet to be developed, although it exists.

1996—Aimee Mullins (b. 1975), a below-the-knee double amputee, is the world record holder in the 100- and 200-meter dashes and long jump at the Paralympic Games. She is also the national record holder for the 200-meter dash.

You know, we can't get out of life alive. We can either die in the bleachers or die on the field. We might as well come down on the field and go for it.
—Les Brown (1912–2001)

Your aptitude may not be apparent in any of the sports or outdoor activities tried to date; however, be assured that it is just lying dormant. It is your duty to yourself to try and try again until you find what moves you. When you do discover your passion, it will become as natural as eating, sleeping, and laughing.

> ***There is nothing that will train leadership, teach how to work
> through conflict, or provide the experience of exhilarating joy and
> accomplishments like team sports. Join anything. The confidence
> that comes from pushing ourselves physically is invaluable.***
> —Kari Blinn (b. 1964), QB, Women's Professional Football League, New England Storm

Self-confidence is gained through sports, but it takes practice to make it look effortless. Expect to be self-conscious and uncoordinated the first few times; most people are when they try something new.

Active play, and enough of it, is missing from many women's days. Women need to take the time to move the way they used to when they were little—strictly for the fun of it and without guilt.

> ***Play is the poetry of the human being.***
> —Jean-Paul Sartre (1905–1980)

Physical exertion makes you feel better. Your body wants to be moved and to move you. It wants to be stretched, challenged, and, above all, appreciated and respected. You need a body that can handle the adventures you dream of, support you in these new activities, and be the means to many hours of outdoor fun.

Marla Runyan (b. 1969) of Eugene, Oregon, became the first legally blind athlete to compete at the 2000 Olympic Games. She placed eighth in the 1500-meter race with a time of 4:08:30.

COMFORTABLE IN HER SKIN

Society suggested "athlete" and "girl" were two different things.
I eventually realized there was no need to separate.
—Francie Larrieu Smith (b. 1952), five-time Olympian,
1998 National Track and Field Hall of Fame inductee

Any active woman has an inherent sense of pride and confidence, and rightly so after spending countless hours in play—she knows her body. She moves with a sense of purpose and worth. Whether she loves to garden or dance, the passion of her play shines through her eyes. Lifting, planting, growing, leaping, spinning, and stretching—she is comfortable in her skin.

CONFIDENCE GAINED

I want to wear jewelry and makeup when I run.
I want to be feminine. It's part of who I am.
—Suzy Favor-Hamilton (b. 1968), two-time Olympian

When a female athlete, either a weekend warrior or a professional, masters a sport, she carries this indisputable competence off the fields or courts and into daily living. She learns that this poise gained is so very valuable in the game of life.

Today's active female does not have to trade in her femininity to play. Our society just needs to see more women moving to whatever moves them. Be a tomboy again, or if you have never been, follow a girl who plays without any apologizes. She will show you the way

I never thought of myself as a tomboy—I'm just a girl who likes sports.
—Shannon Dunn (b. 1971), snowboarder, 2001 Olympic Gold Superpipe, two-time World Halfpipe Champion, 1998 Olympic Bronze Halfpipe, two-time U.S. Open Snowboarding Champion

LIFE'S ENERGY FORCE
There is a vitality, a life force, an energy, a quickening, that is translated through you into action, and because there is only one of you in all time, this expression is unique.
—Martha Graham (1894–1991)

In 1975, Dr. John Hughes and Dr. Hans W. Kosterlitz discovered a new class of brain chemicals, which act just like morphine. Scientists noted that the endorphin levels in the blood rose with exercise. Prolonged, continuous exercise contributes to an increased production and release of endorphins, resulting in a sense of euphoria that has been popularly labeled "runner's high."

This could be the reason why many athletes say that they are addicted to their play.

I play to de-stress and for the fun, endorphin-producing, feel-good kind of tired.
—Leslie Wright, Winston Salem, North Carolina

One of the main endorphins, beta-endorphin, has been shown to lower blood pressure, inhibit pain, and suppress appetite. Whether or not the increase in beta-endorphin is solely responsible for the elevation of mood remains controversial, but regardless, exercise is an excellent approach to improving moods and treating depression. Test this theory for yourself.

Play is to sweat, have fun, and enjoy the time to be energized.
—Maria Kaminski, Bronx, New York

NO SIDE EFFECTS

In a recent study by researchers at Duke University, forty-five minutes of exercise three times a week prescribed for patients older than fifty was just as effective in lessening depression as taking the anti-depression medication sertraline (Zoloft). In fact, after ten months, fewer patients in the exercise group showed relapse for depression.

The beneficial interaction between exercise and feelings of well-being is not a novel idea. The dose of exercise needed to gain improvement in mental health is relatively small. In fact, the same amount of exercise suggested to improve blood pressure or lower triglycerides is equivalent to what is needed to improve mental health. Experts believe that thirty-five minutes of walking or forty-five minutes of bicycling three to four days per week may be all that is needed.

The word "endorphin" is an amalgam of endogenous with morphine,
which means, "a morphine produced naturally in the body."

"It is helpful to think of the brain as a muscle," Dr. John Ratey, a clinical associate professor of psychiatry at Harvard Medical School, "and the best way to maximize the brain is through exercise and movement. Twelve minutes of exercise at 85 percent of your maximum heart rate is like taking a little bit of Prozac and a little bit of Ritalin in a very holistic manner."

Freedom to explore our environment and develop our
bodily abilities is a link to intellectual development.
—Gloria Steinem (b. 1934)

GO OUTSIDE!

Live each season as it passed, breathe the air, drink the drink,
taste the fruit, and resign yourself to the influences of each.
—*Henry David Thoreau (1817–1862)*

Outdoor play is cheap therapy and a guarantee for continuous happiness. Let the weather, change of seasons, the length of daylight inspire you to go outside more often. Play in the snow and the sunshine. See windy, rainy, or icy conditions as your personal summons to discover a new kind of fun in such days. By adopting this attitude of "nothing is going to stop me now," no change in weather will. Louise, my hiking buddy, heads outside every morning in the summer before it gets too hot. Come winter, she waits until after lunch for the sun to warm up the air and the trails. By using the weather as a motivator, she fits play into her days on a regular basis.

*Play is anything to get me outside and doing an
activity that makes me grow and feel healthy.*
——Jenn Reno, Jackson Hole, Wyoming

If it is the mountain that you want to conquer, start with little steps. First, walk its trails in the spring, then by summer, run or walk through the woods. Come autumn, roll out your bike and take to the same trails that you now know so well. With the arrival of winter's first blanket of snow, test out snow shoes and cross-country or alpine skis. Without any rules or expectations—yours or anybody else's—just try.

1988——Stacy Allison (b. 1958) is the first American woman to climb what many consider the most difficult mountain on Earth   Mt. Everest at 29,035 feet above sea level.

PLAY IN NATURE

In the summer of 1996, the American population made the silent yet monumental step from being predominantly rural to being predominantly urban.

Plant a garden of vegetables, flowers, or fruit, or plan a flower garden to be able to pick bouquets throughout all of August. Rake the autumn leaves and jump into the pile. Sweep the patio and walkway and invite neighbors over for a barbecue. Shovel the snow from the driveway and have friends over for hot chocolate and fresh baked cookies. All of this physical activity will do your spirit good, and your interaction with nature will reward you in many ways.

Pine Sauna

Essential oil of pine (pinus sylvestris) has been traditionally used by the
Scandinavians in the sauna or steam bath for its refreshing and antiseptic qualities.
Adopt their custom and bring the essence of outdoors indoors.
Place ten drops in a bowl of hot water inside the sauna. Stir to release the essence.
For a modified steam bath in the shower, fill a plastic spray bottle with seven drops of the oil and
fill with warm water. Shake well, spray the area around you, and breathe deeply.

THE SECRET TO HEALTH

May the road rise to meet you,
may the wind always be at your back,
may the sun shine warm upon your face,
may the rains fall softly upon your fields…
—Irish Blessing

The secret to healthy living is to play well and often, especially outdoors. Think of the people you know who are active. They are rarely sick. They also have an incredible amount of energy and are generally upbeat, happy souls. Decide to join them. Get out the badminton racquets, net, and birdie, or the croquette set. Learn how to play the Italian lawn game of bocce ball or master juggling.

Healthy Reasons to Play

Improve strength.

Increase stamina.

Lower cholesterol.

For the health of your heart.

Balance blood sugar.

Reduce risk of osteoporosis.

Reduce risk of cancer.

Handle hypertension.

Ward off the common cold.

Muscle is a natural fat-burner.

ACTIVE PLAY

Play to me is free-hearted, free-spirited, leave-the-mind-behind fun!
—*Andrea, Granada Hills, California*

I particularly enjoy sports that allow you to vent frustration. Author Annie Dillard voiced the same sentiments when she said, "I remember…walking that famously lonely walk out to the mound, our gravel driveway, to hurl baseballs against the garage wall."

Pick up a golf club and go drive a bucket of balls. Grab a field hockey or lacrosse stick and fire off goals. Get your baseball bat and head off to the local batting cage. Call a friend and meet her at the outdoor racquetball court. Play until your body produces enough endorphins to erase the stress of the day.

Need a little help on your golf game? Play at altitude. The lack of oxygen in the atmosphere will help your ball soar farther than normal, perhaps dropping your score by a few strokes.

The physical effort of throwing can also release the stress of the day quickly. Stop by the toy store on your way to a park or beach and pick up a Frisbee or a boomerang, bring along a baseball or softball—anything to toss around while letting time slip by.

The United States Boomerang Association says the boomerang, originally called a kylie, was used by the Australian aborigines for hunting. Other evidence dates back to the Stone Age where it was found in ancient Egypt, the American Southwest, and Eastern Europe.

Remember how to skip stones? Find a pond or lake and start throwing. The sun's reflection from the water will warm you, and the rays will deliver your daily dose of vitamin D.

According to medical findings, vitamin D is made when our skin is exposed to the sun. Your body needs this vitamin to process calcium, so get your sunshine dosage two to three times a week with ten to fifteen minutes of sunlight and no sunscreen.

THINK OF YOURSELF AS AN ATHLETE

Try Aerobic Sports: walking, cycling, jogging, swimming, step classes, or cross-country skiing

A fitness program without fun will not last a lifetime, or even a summer. Focus on the fun, not the end results measured by scales and calipers. Call your active time "playing." Keep seriousness out of this time—avoid calling it "a workout" or "exercising." Semantics—but it does make a difference.

People rarely succeed unless they have fun in what they are doing.
—*Dale Carnegie (1888–1955)*

One of the biggest mistakes people make when starting to play a sport is they start doing too much too soon and they burn out, get injured, or quit due to achy muscles. Each session should include a warm-up period of at least five minutes, a dynamic portion of a longer duration, and a cool-down period. This bell-curve approach will help prevent injuries.

Cross Play: Include all four types of movement in your play: endurance, strength, balance, and flexibility. This is one sure way to try different sports and activate all your muscles.

Sore Muscle Bath Salts

1 cup of Dead Sea salts (or Epsom salt)

5-8 drops of essential oil of rosemary (rosmarinus officinalis)

Place the salt in a bowl and stir in the essential oil, mixing well with a fork. Place the bath salts in a decorative container with a tight-fitting lid for a day to allow the salts to absorb the essence. Before you use your bath salts, stir again to make sure the oil has been well dispersed. Add 1 cup of bath salts to the bath water just before getting in, and stir to dissolve the salts. Soak in the woody fragrance of rosemary and enjoy the powerful effect this essence has on your muscles.

Think of yourself as an athlete starting now, today. When you make the time to play outdoors, your body will become stronger each and every day. You are building a healthier you inside and out. The fact that you are embracing this new segment of your life and giving it a try is enough to call yourself an athlete.

Try Anaerobic Activities: racquetball, downhill skiing, weight-lifting, mountain biking, sprinting, softball, baseball, soccer, or football—tackle or flag.

SUN PLAY

July is Anti-Boredom Month. Find something new to do.

This summer, leave any inhibitions in the house and go jump into the sandbox with the kids. Play without rules and create your own backyard games. Set up a maze or an obstacle course to challenge the kids' foot/eye coordination as well as yours.

Ice-blocking is equivalent to sled riding but done in August. All you need is a steep, grassy slope and a block of ice. Remember to bring an old towel to place over the ice block, giving you something to hold onto on your wild ride.

WATER PLAY

By means of water we give life to everything.
—The Koran

Water is exhilarating, a necessity for both body and spirit. Be sure to include this element in your quest for fun-filled activities. On your adventure to discover play, return to soaking wet summer pastimes when games were free and the afternoons endless. Wash the car and then start a friendly water balloon battle with whoever is in tossing range. Set up the sprinkler and run through its invigorating shower. If you feel a bit too adult to be having so much fun, invite your kids, the grandkids, someone else's grandkids, or the neighborhood kids. Dedicate one day a week to water levity.

Play is any activity for fun and health.
—Kris Tratiak, Springfield, Massachusetts

Surfing legend Margo Oberg won the Western Surfing Association amateur title at the age of fifteen, just four years after she started surfing. This title earned her a place in the World Champions. In 1968, she amazed everyone, capturing the world crown. Today, she still can be seen shredding on Kauai.

Make regular pilgrimages to the water's edge. At sunrise, a lake's water is most like a smooth sheet of glass. This is your invitation to go waterskiing, swimming, canoeing, or fishing. The early morning hours at the beach are best for surfing, snorkeling, or scuba diving. When the winds kick up in the afternoon, accept this change in the elements as a way to make the entire day perfect and go out for sail, be it on a boat or a board.

The earth is a watery place—approximately 70 percent of its surface is covered in H_2O. Go find your golden pond. Return frequently and watch as water washes away the worries of your world.

1926—Gertrude Ederle swims across the English Channel. In America, women who removed their stockings to swim are arrested for swimming nude.

SEE JANE RUN

According to researchers at University of Irvine of California, College of Medicine, your daily jog may do more than keep you fit   it may also prevent the deterioration of brain cells that can lead to Alzheimer's disease.

Running has given me the courage to start, the determination to keep trying, and the child-like spirit to have fun along the way. Run often and run long, but never outrun your joy of running.
—*Julie Isphording (b.1961), ran in the first marathon event at the Olympics when it was added for women in 1984*

Doris Heritage, five-time world cross-country champion, had the courage to run during the fifties when girls at her high school were not allowed on the track. "When you went out running by yourself, people said nasty things and threw footballs at you." The six-time world record holder now uses her runs as a sign of freedom and a time to be thankful for life's beauty.

Stay Outside!

If your sense of direction is one area of play that needs some training, test out the latest wilderness gadget called a global positioning system (GPS). The GPS, originally used by the U.S. Department of Defense, is now readily available (with a reasonable price tag) to get you out in the woods and home again.

This autumn season, check out a new park, trail, or meadow. Bring along your significant other or the family dog, and enjoy the fresh air together. Breathe in the aroma of fresh pine, feel the caress of lighter, purer air, and see the brilliant exhibition of the flora's hues and tones. The chorus of songs only found in nature will lull your busy mind into a state of peacefulness with each step.

Bring memories and the songs of nature indoors with you.
Check the selections under "nature" at your local music store.

When was the last time you really looked at the sky and studied those cotton-ball puffs floating by or morphing into an elephant? How long has it been since you noticed its changing colors as the day turns from early to late afternoon? Go get a kite and allow your new form of play to turn your attention and appreciation skyward. It does not have to be an expensive or complicated one. In fact, your flying machine of choice could be a cheap balsa wood airplane with one-step assembly where you simply slide the wings into place and let it fly.

Lunchtime provides the perfect opportunity to explore this vast space. Pack a picnic complete with a tablecloth, cloth napkin, and your new toy—in place of dessert. Release your kite into the azure sky or send your plane toward the heavens.

You will be amazed at how slowly time will pass when you deliberately let go of it.

The first kite is believed to have flown more than two thousand years ago in China.
A parallel belief gives recognition to the Malaysians or Indonesians
who were known to make kites from leaves.

After Daylight Savings Time rolls by in October, continue to go mountain biking with your new toys: a light for your helmet and bike. On your first night ride, take a few friends and start on a trail that you know well.

SNOW PLAY

Scientists estimate that ten million Americans suffer from seasonal
depression, and twenty-five million more develop milder versions.

As the weather turns colder, keep yourself motivated, not hibernating, so you will not have to stop and start your fitness program each year. Make the decision to play outside this half of the year, too. With each passing month, you will see your mood improve and your energy increase.

During my first winter in Steamboat Springs, Colorado, I reluctantly hung up my road and mountain bikes when my front yard became a permanent white carpet. I tried riding the stationary bike at the gym; I lasted a half hour, speed-reading four magazines before I quit out of boredom. At home, I rode my wind trainer while watching European bike races on television, but the normal household distractions—dishes, laundry, piles of stuff—pulled me off my bike in about the same amount of time that boredom did.

About a month into winter, I discovered that I could still mountain bike on the snow-covered trails. Now instead of missing my rides for six months of the year, I can still to do what I love—at least when the temperature is above 20 degrees Fahrenheit.

Try skijor—a new way to get into winter with your dog. Together, you cross-country ski while your pet helps you along by pulling like a sled dog.

Look forward to the changes in the seasons and prepare for the upcoming fun. In anticipation of opening day at the ski resort, wax your skis or get them into the shop for repairs. Unearth the toboggan, sleds, and snow tubes for guaranteed fun this winter on any hill painted white.

Head to the lakes to ice fish, and when the local pond is completely frozen over, go in search of your ice skates. Bring along brooms and a ball to start a modified game of ice hockey or play crack the whip. Afterwards, enjoy the camaraderie around a bonfire with roasted hot dogs and marshmallows.

If you love to jog or walk, but find it too chilly to do either November through March, test out snow-shoeing, cross-country skiing, or ice skating. With the new techno fabrics and a little extra movement, you will heat up before long and find yourself looking forward to these new ways to get outside during the winter months.

Winter Play Remedies

Mall Walks. Many shopping malls nationwide will allow you (and your group) to walk prior to the stores opening—if not, walk during the store hours.

Join a Health Club. Meet new friends and have a designated place to go.

Dive In. Water aerobics, water yoga, or water ballet will keep you splashing all winter long in an indoor heated pool.

Home Exercise Equipment. During the winter, your new toy may be the best way to keep you healthy and happy.

Now when I'm on the ice, I think of the pure joy of skating. Last year, I was skating for nothing. This year, I'm skating for the love of it, for the fun.
—Michelle Kwan (b. 1980), first woman to record a perfect score of 6.0 at the U.S. Championships, 1998 Olympic Silver

Snowboarding Tip: In addition to wearing a helmet, try a pair of wrist guards over your gloves.

❧

Winter Playing Tips

Head into the Wind. Start your jaunt outside by going into the headwind. This slight resistance will heat up your body faster, plus, on the way back, the tailwind will propel you home quicker.

Drink Plenty of Liquids. Even in the winter, you still need water to prevent dehydration. Test out the water packs that can be worn on your back, under a ski jacket, or around the waist.

Be Visible. Wear reflective clothing and shoes, or add your own reflective tape to your outer jacket or vest. If you cycle at dusk, add a blinking light to your bike and a headlamp to your helmet to be seen by drivers.

Stay Toasty. Since most of your body heat is loss through your head, don a cap. Also check out the latest in technological active wear. These fabrics will wick sweat and moisture from your skin and keep you warmer than cotton or wool.

INDOOR MOTION

There are short cuts to happiness, and dancing is one of them.
—Vicki Baum (1888–1960)

Instead of being cooped up inside with nothing to do, check out a few sport videos to keep your motivation and movement on high. Stop by your local video rental store and dare your body to try something new.

A fusion of hip hop and jazz music, such as Robert Randolph and the Family Band's Live at the Wetland, *will keep you moving indoors.*

Remember, Ginger Rogers did everything Fred Astaire did, but she did it backwards and in high heels.
—*Faith Whittlesey (b. 1939)*

Dancing is said to be the most moving and most beautiful of all of the arts. Take a dance class   salsa, classical ballet, tango, the waltz, rumba—however you best move your feet. Get out there on the dance floor again—your body wants to move to the rhythm of music.

Dance, even if you have nowhere to do it but your living room.
—*Kurt Vonnegut, Jr. (b. 1922)*

Kicks, Hits, and Throws

My brother was an important influence at the beginning of my career,
and he is still my biggest fan. My parents basically said nothing, so
I guess I did what I wanted. I needed an outlet for my emotions.
—Lucia Rijker (b. 1967), undefeated female kickboxer, 1997–98
European Champion, Current U.S. record 14-0

The muscles in your body, just like your brain, need to be used daily. Martial arts, Pilates, and yoga stimulate the mind and body in a different direction than sports. Each move or posture is an opportunity to slow the mind, and permits you to be fully in the moment while evoking a relaxation response.

Martial arts such as tai chi or jujitsu teach respect for the body, build strength, and improve balance, as well as encourage meditation.

Be Safe: Self-defense classes are essential for all women.
Sign up for a class with your daughter(s) and friends.

Join the Excitement

Everyone is an athlete, there are just those
who are training and those who aren't.
—George Sheehan M.D. (1918–1993)

One sure step in the right direction to add fun, play, and excitement to your days is to volunteer. Instead of running at your first 5K, help pass out water at the support stations.

You might be surprised at the diverse ability level of those who reach out for a splash of water. In fact, why not start to run/walk the same day that you sign up to volunteer? No pressure—just an opportunity to see if you can. Maybe next year when the race date rolls around again, you will be the runner accepting the cup of water.

The same advice is applicable for those who want to challenge their current level of ability. Train with someone who has completed the upcoming race. Go witness the event first so you will be able to set your training tactics and schedule accordingly.

Energizing Leg Massage: Mix five drops of peppermint or spearmint essential oil to three tablespoons of grapeseed or sweet almond carrier oil. Swirl gently to mix and then massage your legs.

Think of reasons to play, not excuses not to. Post this list (or draft your own) to encourage your daily dose of active play:

Thirty Reasons To Play!

1. Explore!
2. Time just for me
3. Connect with old friends
4. Make new friends
5. Have extra energy
6. Learn a new skill
7. Expand my interests
8. Expand my world
9. Think more clearly
10. Have fun
11. Sleep better
12. Be in a better mood
13. Be happy
14. Be healthier
15. Be with my dog
16. Be strong
17. Increase my strength
18. Be independent
19. Be confident
20. Time to problem solve
21. Reduce stress
22. Be with God

23. Be in nature

24. Get a suntan

25. Be me!

26. Sweat out toxins

27. Eat healthier

28. Renew my enthusiasm for life

29. Be powerful

30. Because I want to!

According to Reuters Health, running may give your brain a workout, too. A new study finds that individuals consistently score higher on intellectual tests after embarking on a running program.

WINNING

Whoever said, "It is not whether you won or lost," probably lost.
—*Martina Navratilova (b. 1956)*

1999—Mia Hamm, U.S. Soccer Player of the Year from 1993–98 and forward on the 1996 Olympic Gold U.S. soccer team, becomes the world's leading goal-scorer among both men and women.

Winning encourages confidence; it pushes you farther than you may have imagined. Winning shows your play was on track and proved you had the discipline to go the distance. It means you gave it your best and your best was good enough to be the very best.

In wheelchair sports, people thought athletes with disabilities were courageous and inspirational. They never give them credit for simply being competitive.
—*Jean Driscoll (b. 1966), Olympian, Paralympian*

1964—Mary Kathryn "Mickey" Wright entered the Hall of Fame of Women's Golf with fifty-eight wins, including eleven majors and five Vare Trophies.

Aim to win because winning feels great. Shoot to better your personal times from previous races, or go for first place in your age category or the entire race. Pick up a flyer for a half marathon, cross country mountain bike race, or a biathlon. Work backwards from the race date to best achieve your goal, but above all else, enjoy your journey; it will make winning so much more rewarding.

Training Ideas

A-to-B Routes: Head out in one direction and arrange to have someone pick you up at a designated time. Or run to a friend's house and ask for a ride home.

Circuits: Use these preset courses to do loops or laps at the community or neighbor's pool, the high school track, around the neighborhood block, or out on the hiking trails. Circuits are a perfect solution when you do not have a lot of time, but want to be outside.

Impromptu: With no direction in mind, just go. Let your body take you where it wants to.

Time: Watch the clock and go for ten, fifteen, or thirty minutes, then turn around and go home.

Distance: Do not watch the clock, just the miles. Go for one hundred yards or meters, ten miles or kilometers, then turn around and go home.

I ride with the men in local and regional races.
If it's a road race, I'll do the men's race and then the women's;
if it's a mountain bike race, I'll just do the men's.
—Alison Dunlap (b. 1970), cross-country mountain bike racer, 2001 World Champion, five-time National Cyclo-cross Champion, two-time Olympian for both mountain and road cycling

Tell-tale Signs of Dehydration
Lack of energy
Impaired concentration
Headaches
Irritability
Fatigue

Spice up that eight glasses of your daily water allotment with slices of orange, lemon, lime, or kiwi, or drop in a chunk of seedless watermelon or a big juicy strawberry to slightly flavor your required beverage. Splash your glass with a bit of fruit juice for variety.

COMPETE

This section is for those who are ready to meet the challenge. If you have built a competent base of proficiency at a sport for a length of time, step up to the next level of experience: "competition." It is not a dirty word; women can say it and should with pride. Winning is an absolutely wonderful feeling. Every woman should experience it many times in her life.

1993—Julieanne Louise Krone (b. 1963) made horse-racing history as the first woman to win the 125 running of the Belmont Stakes, one of the U.S. Triple Crown races. One of the most celebrated jockeys, Krone competed with more than 3,300 trips to the winner's circle, and in 2001 was the first female jockey elected to the Thoroughbred Racing Hall of Fame.

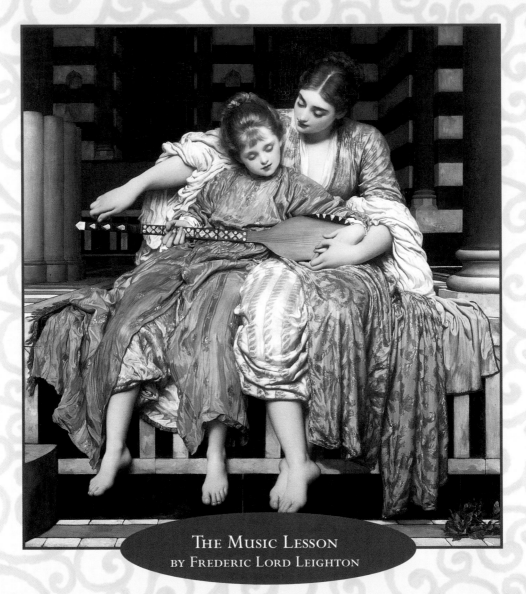

THE MUSIC LESSON
BY FREDERIC LORD LEIGHTON

CHAPTER SIX

Creative Expression

ART, PROSE, AND SONG

What is passion? It is surely the becoming of a person.
—*John Boorman (b. 1933)*

How can some people create with what appears to be an effortless wave of the hand? Creative expression is a gift. It is also a passion. It is much practice, but lives within all of us.

Discover what you are.
—*Henry Ward Beecher (1813–1887)*

Express and create whatever your artistic desire—for yourself. You are the only audience that matters. Do not listen to your internal art critic. Besides, without practice, everyone's talent dies. If it makes you happy, makes you smile, reduces stress, and adds an element of tranquillity to your life, reserve two or three hours every week for your new passion.

Awaken the dominant self who says she is too busy for her creative life. Creative play is good for the mind and body. Katharine Hepburn began painting in the 1930s. "I still have my first two paintings. I still love to paint. I find it relaxing."

POSSIBILITIES

When we are relaxed and comfortable, anything is possible.

Ancient Greeks and Romans believed in the therapeutic benefits of a mineral bath. Take to the waters as these earlier philosophers, musicians, writers, and artists once did, and soak in the pure silence of mental bantering. Let the ideas rise and fall as you ponder your next masterpiece or stanza.

Christen your bathroom—your new spa destination—with pampering items to encourage relaxation and creative birth of new ideas. This is your tranquil place to go, to be alone and think. Furnish your sanctuary with scented candles, a small vase of fragrant flowers, instrumental music, fluffy towels, a carafe of water and glass, and essences for the tub's waters. Visit frequently for inspiration and the renewal of your creative self.

The word "spa" is originally from a resort town in Belgium whose healing mineral waters were discovered in the fourteenth century. Bath, England, is also famous for its waters, and was first established as a spa by the Romans in A.D 44. Add these two destinations to your travel wish list after you soak awhile at home.

We act as though comfort and luxury were the chief requirements of life when all that we need to make us happy is something to be enthusiastic about.
——*Charles Kingsley (1819–1875)*

The start of a new year is an excellent time to begin a new hobby or return to your art. Sip a hot beverage and review the Sunday paper to see what new exhibitions are coming to nearby museums and what plays or dance shows are opening this month. Plan a trip out of the cold to a warmer climate and visit places germane to your creative expression.

Give me a museum and I will fill it.
——*Pablo Picasso (1881–1973)*

Maté *or Argentinean tea, drunk in carved-out gourds with a straw, is very popular in South America and is taken in place of regular tea. The leaves of the* Ilex paraguariensis, *a plant similar to holly, are ground to make this traditional beverage. Avoid letting* maté *steep too long because it does contain caffeine and may become bitter. Enjoy hot and add a slice of lemon or orange or a touch of cinnamon, nutmeg, or ground ginger if you wish.*

BE BOLD

Fortune favors the bold.
—*Virgil (70–19 B.C.)*

French artist Rosa Bonheur smoked in public, refused to ride sidesaddle, and bobbed her hair short. She favored men's attire, but was forced to obtain an official police authorization to be allowed to wear trousers and a smock. To better understand the subjects of her paintings, she visited slaughterhouses. Bonheur's unconventional style created a myth about her during her lifetime; however, this most renowned painter of animals definitely knew her subject.

They [the critics] thought I was a Surrealist, but I wasn't.
I never painted my dreams. I painted my reality.
—*Frida Kahlo (1907–1954)*

Write about what you know. Paint what you love. Create from the heart. Research, study, and learn about your passion from others: local talent, old-world masters, and instructors.

Explore new methods and delve into your time with new eyes. Build your creative foundation with time devoted to practice and mix your days with education and intuition.

I want to dance for everyone in the world.
—*Anna Pavlova (1881–1931)*

1979—The American Academy and Institute of
Arts and Letters inducts sculptor Louise Nevelson.

Return to a form of expression that you loved as a child. Note how your spirit receives an immediate boost of happiness just from the memory of it. Or choose to try something that you have always dreamed of. If you can picture yourself doing it, you can do it. Go. Time is waiting for you to create.

Keep true to the dreams of thy youth.
—*Johann Christopher Friedrich von Schiller (1759–1805)*

The Top Ten List for Creating

10. Learn something new.
 9. Perfect a skill.
 8. Play in colors.
 7. Experiment with textures.
 6. Savor the five senses.
 5. Be in a happy mood.
 4. Alleviate stress.
 3. Create with your hands.
 2. Develop commitment.
 1. Smile more!

FOR THE LOVE OF PLAY: WORK

Play is enjoyment of an activity and includes art, recreation, sports, and in my case, "work," that is photography, reading, research, and creative expression.
—Linda Litteral, Waukegan, Illinois

One of the interesting handwritten notes received on the back of my survey said: "Due to history and other circumstances of my growing up in Eastern Europe, I never had a childhood to learn the meaning of "play"; I only did later in adulthood. It is the greatest gift of my life and I have found both 'physical' and 'creative' play as a photographer."

Play has become a way of life that this woman intends to keep in all of her days. For her and many others, work can be play if it is kept as a passion.

1919—Architect Julia Morgan (b. 1872) is hired by William Randolph Hearst to design and build all of the structures and houses at his ranch in San Simeon, California, including La Casa Grande with more than one hundred rooms, a garage to hold twenty-five cars, and indoor and outdoor swimming pools.

FOR LOVE OF THE WRITTEN WORD

Reading is to the mind what exercise is to the body.
—Richard Steele (1672–1729)

Researcher Peter Huttenlocher at the University of Chicago says, "The brain is like a block of marble and we have to use outside experiences to shape it into a working organ."

The love of the written word will allow your creative soul to appreciate great books and travel the world without leaving the comfort of your home. Savor the many wonderful books written by women about travel and their experiences of living among other cultures, but be careful. Their contagious enthusiasm and descriptive words may have you packing for a distant island in the South Pacific, or at least pondering a house swap with a European family next summer.

1952—Rachel Carson receives the National Book Award
for her nonfiction book The Sea Around Us.

Check out the library's reading club and take to devouring books. The lively discussion that will undoubtedly ensue every month can bring a greater meaning to your readings and your passion. You will be introduced to new genres and authors who you will wish you had met sooner in life.

While pursuing your favorite author's latest plot, try a new concoction—Mint Licorice Infusion—an excellent beverage to sip hot.

Mint Licorice Infusion

3 leaves of spearmint or peppermint

A pinch of fennel

A pinch of aniseed

A pinch of ground licorice

Lemon pinwheels

Boil 1½ cups of water and pour over the ingredients, except lemons. Steep for three minutes. Strain and serve with a slice of lemon. Cautionary note: since this infusion is stimulating, it is not recommended for those with high blood pressure.

If it is your desire to become "conversationally bilingual," you maybe be satisfied by reading armchair travel books. Many of these authors sprinkle their English writing with enough of the native language to teach the basics: "Hello," "Good-bye," and "Where is the water closet?"

> **Reading makes immigrants of us all. It takes us away from home, but more important, it finds homes for us everywhere.**
> —*Hazel Rochman (b. 1938)*

Others (like myself) may need a structured class to pick up the intricacies of the foreign tongue. Let foreign words become a new way to play for you. Collect coffee table books or calendars of your favorite lands and make plans to visit your dream destination.

To set the right ambiance for your reading hour, add the essence of clary sage
(salvia sclaria) to a light bulb ring burner, taking care not to drip on the bulb.
This circular ceramic or metal diffuser sits atop the bulb, and with the heat generated
over time, slowly emits a sweet, nutty, herbaceous aroma about the room.

Through the appreciation of great authors and equally wonderful stories grows the love of the written word, and through this fascination with prose develops the potential writer. Avid reading creates writers; there is no way around this fact.

> **If there's a book you really want to read, but it hasn't been written yet, then you must write it.**
> —Toni Morrison (b. 1931)

April is National Poetry Month. Take the next thirty days and introduce yourself
to Maya Angelou, Elizabeth Barrett Browning, Edna St. Vincent Millay,
or other female poets whose prose intrigues you.

Express your creative self in writing poetry, haiku, or the next great American short story. Locate a writing group and attend one of its gatherings. If this group of creative minds has not come together yet, start one. Seek out other writers—they will be the unconditional support that your creative self needs in this solitary pursuit.

*The writer should never be ashamed of staring.
There is nothing that does not require her attention.*
—Flannery O'Connor (1925–1964)

*1950—Gwendolyn Brooks is the first black woman to win the
Pulitzer Prize for her collection of poems, Annie Allen.*

≈

Music Appreciation
Without music, life is a journey through a desert.
—Pat Conroy (b. 1945)

*According to a recent Gallup poll, America is a country full of music-
makers, with approximately 113 million Americans over the age of
twelve who claim to be current or former music makers.*

≈

From Grand Ole Opry country music, swing, big band,
reggae, and ragtime to jazz, new age, folk, Celtic, and the
blues—any genre that can reserve precious moments for
play is wonderful. Whether your time involves going to an
outdoor bluegrass festival, relaxing at an intimate jazz

lounge, or hearing a Baroque chamber quartet play in the botanical gardens, you are taking the time to appreciate creative expression. Collect it, support it, and let it live loudly within your life.

Your passion as an appreciation will burn just as bright as those who make the music.

Sometimes I throw sound around the band like paint and other times I play and feel as if I was carving silence like a sculptor.
—Jane Ira Bloom (b. 1955), soprano saxophonist / composer

India Arie's Acoustic Soul *is perhaps what your creative self wants to appreciate this afternoon. With guitar play by India, strings instead of synthesizers, and drums rather than drum machines—her music is true inspiration.*

MUSICAL EXPRESSION

Playing my flute and clarinet [improvisations]
is more play to me because it is creative.
—*Diana Simon from Rochester, New York*

Stretch your mind and time and compose music or write lyrics. Do whatever it takes to allow your musical soul to be heard. Start a band in the garage just for fun. Join the church's choir or the holiday carolers in December.

In 1942, Viola Smith, a veteran drummer of seventeen years, sent shock waves through the readership of Down Beat *by extolling the existence of female jazz musicians. Smith said, "[Women] could sit in any jam session and hold their own."*

If you expressed your musical talent as a child, but have not tapped its reserve in your adult life, why not re-ignite your passion?

Want to learn to play an instrument? Hire a teacher and learn to play the guitar, pennywhistle, harp, violin, steel drums, or take singing lessons. Let your musical voice be heard.

Singing songs like "The Man I Love" or "Porgy" is no more work than sitting down and eating Chinese roast duck, and I love roast duck.
—*Billie Holiday (1915–1959)*

PLAY A PART

I can remember taking my nine-month-old daughter to see a college production of *The Wizard of Oz*. I was certain that she would not make it to the play's intermission, but I craved the magic of theater. When the lights went down and the red velvet curtain parted, she did not move for the next forty-five minutes. With her green eyes transfixed on center stage, we stayed for the entire production. Afterwards, my only wish was that she could tell me what she thought of the show.

*1954—The first black opera singer to sign with the Metropolitan
Opera in New York City is contralto Marian Anderson.*

The exhilaration of a musical, an opera, or play is quite contagious. If you have never seen a live performance—go. Be a part of theater arts. You may be moved to write a piece for the stage or audition for the town's theater production.

The Camino Real Playhouse in San Juan Capistrano, California, hosts the *ShowOff!* playwriting festival every year. The ten-minute plays are due by June 15 with the top seven plays performed in October. Challenge yourself—writing a ten-page screenplay might be harder than you think, but definitely worth the attempt.

Any way you choose to participate, you will be making room for this new expression to live in your life.

A film is—or should be—more like music than like fiction.
It should be a progression of moods and feelings. The theme,
what's behind the emotion, the meaning, all that comes later.
—Stanley Kubrick (1928–1999)

Become a film fanatic and study the greats to write your own screenplay. Review American flicks to contrast with the pace and themes of foreign films. Make gourmet popcorn and renew your appreciation of the silver screen, both new films and the classics. With your love for moving pictures, travel, learn, and enjoy your creative time in the dark.

Appreciation

To have read the greatest work of any great poet, to have beheld
or heard the greatest work of any great painter or musician,
is a possession added to the best things in life.
—Algernon Charles Swinburne (1837–1909)

Step up close to a masterpiece and see each of the artist's brush strokes. Close your eyes and listen to all of the layers of an orchestra as one instrument rises above the others and then blends in. Read aloud from one of your favorite books and hear the voices of the characters speak from the pages. Feel the handiwork of a skilled potter, loom weaver, or willow furniture maker.

The fastest way to develop an appetite for a passion is to appreciate it. Read about it, collect it, and then do it. However, you can only learn so much by observation. Eventually you want to experience creative expression for yourself, even if your art never leaves your studio or typewriter.

ORGANIZATION

I learned…that inspiration does not come like a bolt, nor is it kinetic, energetic striving, but it comes into us slowly and quietly and all the time, though we must regularly and every day give it a little chance to start flowing, prime it with a little solitude and idleness.
—Brenda Ueland (1892–1986)

Organize your life to include a window of creative expression in your busy days. Design your own retreat and fill it with tools for play. If your home does not have any available rooms, take over a corner in the guest room, kitchen, office, along the hallway, in the foyer, or garage.

A woman must have money and a room of her own if she is to write fiction.
—Virginia Woolf (1882–1941)

Essential oil of cinnamon (cinnamomum zeylanicum) is useful to fight depression and fatigue. In your studio, add it to a bowl of potpourri to spice up your mood.

Once springtime has warmed up your corner of the world, consider playing outside. Clear off the picnic table, or set up a spot on the porch or patio.

Make your passion portable, and use boxes, baskets, or buckets to transport your art. Decorate these containers that house your supplies and sources of inspiration, and make their display "art." Now play can be wherever you are.

Music is the divine way to tell beautiful, poetic things to the heart.
—*Pablo Casals (1876–1973)*

Afro Celt Sound System Volume 3: Further in Time
is an excellent, upbeat musical collection to keep you creating.

INSPIRATION

If you stuff yourself full of poems, essays, plays, stories, novels, films, comic strips, magazines, music, you automatically explode every morning like Old Faithful. I have never had a dry spell in my life, mainly because I feed myself well, to the point of bursting. I wake up early and hear my morning voices leaping around in my head like jumping beans. I get out of bed to trap them before they escape.
—Ray Bradbury (b. 1920)

Sandalwood (santalum album) or cedarwood (cedrus atlantica) are considered to possess properties that are opening and grounding. Either essential oil may assist you in settling into your creative time. Light a stick or cone of incense to release its magical essence and see what transpires.

Creative expression, the permission to create, should be a part of every woman's life. Find inspiration in nature and take your art, music, reading, or writing outdoors as often as possible. Your creative expression is guaranteed to blossom under the energizing glow of the sun.

Hike the yellow aspen-lined trails of the Rockies. Take along your camera or paints to capture nature in your own expression. Fill yourself up with so many new inventive ideas that once your imaginative juices start flowing again, it will be impossible to stop them.

Creative Sparks

1. Take a different way home.
2. Become a people watcher. Take notes.
3. Ask questions.
4. Make a room or take space for your creative play.
5. Study or learn from others.
6. Experiment in other forms of your medium.
7. Listen to different genres of music.
8. Read unusual magazines or newspapers.
9. Try exotic or international foods.
10. Watch foreign movies.
11. Travel anywhere new.
12. Start a weekly creative club with others.
13. Keep a picture file for inspiration.

*German artist, Maria Sibylla Merian's (1647–1717) father and stepfather
both housed an abundant collection of prints, paintings, and books,
which Maria was exposed to as a young, budding artist.*

Imagination is more important than knowledge.
—*Albert Einstein (1879–1955)*

You never know where the next idea will come from, but be prepared to capture it. Stash a small tablet, disposable camera, or sketch pad in your bag or briefcase for those unpredictable flashes of inspiration. Your life is a constant source for your future expressions—live with open eyes and ears.

> **The world is but a canvas to the imagination.**
> —*Henry David Thoreau (1817–1862)*

EXPECTATIONS

Berenice Abbott (1898–1991) began expressing her artistic abilities through sculpture in America, but left for Paris where she established her own portrait studio, photographing many of the celebrated literary and artistic figures of her time. During her lifetime, this international photographer also had claims to being an inventor, archivist, and historian.

Surround yourself with greatness. Its constant presence will seep over into your realm. Read the great authors, the classics, the award-winners, and the bestsellers, if you want to be a great writer. Study the old-world masters if your true calling is painting. Find a mentor, a personal trainer, or college professor interested in your pursuit. With their assistance, you cannot help but be great.

Expression

It takes courage to be creative. Just as soon as you
have an idea, you are a minority of one.
—E. Paul Torrance (b. 1925)

Submit your slides to a local art festival. Burn a CD and send your latest tracks off to a music contest. Polish your prose and enter a thousand-words-or-less essay challenge. Competition sets a deadline for creative types who would rather just enjoy the journey. This year, pick one contest, circle its deadline date on your calendar, and get to "playing."

The artist has one function—to affirm and glorify life.
—W. Edward Brown (1830–1897)

Music can be very instrumental in the process of creation.
Try Verve: Remix Various Artists: Jazz *for a new dose of creativity today.*

Grow Your Creativity

Join. Discover a regional group, a national association, or international organization. Reach outside of your own world to renew your inspiration.

Attend. Attend a convention or trade show about your passion.

Donate. Keep your art alive. Give it to a charitable organization's silent auction or the public radio station for their membership drive. Accept the recognition and free publicity, but do not forget to take the tax deduction.

Volunteer. Become a docent at the local art museum, help at the public library, or play an instrument for the church.

Teach. Share your enthusiasm and teach Saturday classes, teach at the local schools, or offer private lessons.

Lecture. Offer to be a guest speaker at colleges, for civil groups, or at charity functions.

We are the heroes of our own stories.
—*Mary McCarthy (1912–1989)*

THE CHEAT WITH THE ACE OF CLUBS
BY GEORGES DE LA TOUR

CHAPTER SEVEN

Mind Play

FUN AND GAMES

Follow your bliss.
—*Joseph Campbell (1904–1987)*

Every woman needs to return to hobbies to fill her creative self rather than allowing endless work to block that breathing space. According to Betty Freidan, author of *The Feminine Mystique*, housework (and paperwork) will expand exponentially to fill the time allocated. Do not let it happen. Budget adequate time to do what needs to be done, delegate, or subtract a thing to do today—or just say "no." With 168 hours in every week, reserve a mere two or three hours for fun and games.

FOR THE LOVE OF ARTS AND CRAFTS

Find something you're passionate about and keep tremendously interested in it.
—*Julia Child (b. 1912)*

Hobbies and crafts require the use of your hands to release your creative spirit and invite the mind along for the journey. There are at least 1,001 ideas to try and as many great books to show you how. From jewelry to maskmaking to using a needle to knit, needlepoint, crochet, or hook a rug; from weaving on a loom to scrapbooking; your hands will never be bored again. With a hobby like candle-, soap-, or dollmaking, calligraphy or decoupage, the end result—your art—can be shared at birthdays, holidays, or any occasion.

Ikebana, *the practice of arranging flowers by rules, was originally practiced only by men. The two types of arrangements,* Heika *and* Moribana, *required different disciplines, yet both are very creative and relaxing processes, allowing the practitioner to express her temperament and unwind at the same time.*

FOR THE LOVE OF COLLECTIBLES

"Nearly one-fourth of American collectors used the Internet in the past year to gather information about their collections or to chat with other collectors," according to Pam Danziger, president of Unity Marketing.

A new hobby of collecting will send you off on a life-long quest. Roam your world or visit distant lands in search of rare books, fine or pop artwork, or seashells and driftwood to be found on faraway sands.

Frequent flea markets, Internet auctions, or multi-dealer fairs. Join a collector's club to grow your passion of found objects both new and antique, be it Chinese parchment scrolls, gnomes, or all things made of pewter. If you are a numismatist, you may enjoy attending a trade show or convention with foreign currency.

Collect and display your creative passion to give it as much space in your life as you can. As your taste changes, so should your collection. Trays are a good means to display your smaller collections, allowing you to move or rearrange them easily. Enjoy the evolution of your collection as well as the growth of your creative self.

For the Love of Food

Kitchen Aromatherapy: Essential oil of orange (citrus sinensis) is widely used in food.
After dinner tonight, try a chocolate-orange confectionery.

My kitchen is a mystical place, a kind of temple for me. It is a place where the surfaces seem to have significance, where the sounds and odors carry meaning that transfers from the past to the future.
—*Pearl Bailey (1918–1990)*

From everyday cooking to bread-making, cookie-baking or cake-decorating, chances are that you already possess a love of some form of food preparation (one friend of mine doesn't like to cook, but loves to make salads with fresh ingredients or magnificent fruit salads with every variety of exotic fruit she can find). Take the step to the next level and let your food play become a culinary art.

Taste the creations of a gourmet cook, a professional pastry chef, or a master bread-baker and be inspired to create gourmet dishes using the freshest ingredients. If you've never baked, try baking Tollhouse cookies, discover the joys of kneading bread, or experiment with a bread machine. Join a gourmet cooking club and take a peek behind the scenes at five-star restaurants. Invite chefs to speak and teach at your gatherings or to demonstrate their favorite recipes.

Experiment on your own. Learn from cookbooks how to make ethnic foods and be sure to play appropriate music during your study session. Afterwards, wear traditional garb for the feast.

> **There is no love sincerer than the love of food.**
> —*George Bernard Shaw (1856–1950)*

If you are stirring up a Cajun dish of jambalaya, listen to Alligator Stomp Volume Two *by Rhino. Cooking Italian? Turn on* Italian Musical Odyssey *by Putumayo to be serenaded by pure Italian folk music, from Sicily to Venice.*

FUN AND GAMES

Happiness comes only when we push our brains and hearts
to the farthest reaches of which we are capable.
—Leo C. Rosten (1908–1997)

Memory games such as puzzles, Trivial Pursuit, and card or board games can help the mind stay fit and healthy. Use your intellectual muscle today. Reading keeps the brain processing and thinking, so pick up a good book, work on a crossword puzzle, or tell jokes to make someone else (and yourself) laugh.

Authors Lawrence Katz and Manning Rubin of *Keep Your Brain Alive* write, "In much the same way that you can maintain your physical well-being, you can take charge of your mental health and fitness."

What will incite your mind? Is it a former childhood pastime such as backyard summer activities, board games, or puzzles? This mental stimulation will do your whole body good. Your mind wants to participate and laugh again.

Awaken the tired self who says she is too busy for fun. In rediscovering your authentic self, the person who is happiest when doing what feels right and natural, you may unearth a former passion for mind play: a hobby, arts and crafts, or just hours of fun and games.

A study in the July 2001 issue of Health Psychology *stated that exercising (playing)*
for just ten minutes a day can significantly improve our mental outlook.

NO MEMBERSHIP REQUIRED
Play brings you joyously into the present moment
and produces contagious smiles.
—*Peggy Mulhilvil, Kansas City, Missouri*

Ever since color television entered America's living rooms circa 1966, family board game night has slowly become extinct. In fact, finding your dusty stash of old board games might be as hard as finding the remote. Still, send out a search and rescue party and then invite your family, friends, or roommates to join you.

Start your own "Players' Club" without any membership dues; just rotate the location for each game. Invite a few wild women over to compete in a wicked game of *Monopoly*.

When summer rolls around with its extended sunsets, move game night outside. Take along a quilt and a couple of pillows, too. It probably would not hurt to bribe the crowd with a tall pitcher of lemonade and a big bowl of popcorn either. For a new spin on old-time lemonade, freeze pitted cherries in ice cubes and float in the pitcher.

1924—Elizabeth Phillips creates the early version of Monopoly *called The Landlord's Game.*

With the arrival of snow, send an invitation to another family, suggesting that they trudge through the knee-deep powder to your house every Saturday night for a lively game of *Life*. Encourage them with a promise of hot apple cider upon arrival and a car ride home if they win. Good friends and good times always have a way of warming up even the most bitterly cold days.

Heatstroke *by Hawke is an upbeat, jazzy compilation made for winter board game parties. This blissful cover of smiles, sun, and blue water will lead you to a New Orleans club with horns, bongos, whistles, and many vocalists who deliver this distinct tropical beat.*

Host a Murder Mystery Party with instructions in the invitation to dress the part of their assigned character. If the game of choice for the afternoon is *Clue*, assign roles ahead of time, so that Colonel Mustard can then find his monocular in time and Miss Scarlet can borrow a red dress.

Before the party starts, perfume your living room or great room with clary sage (*salvia sclaria*) or jasmine (*jasminum officinale*) to create a heady, "feel good" ambiance.

Sweet orange (*citrus sinensis*), lemongrass (*cymbopogon citratus*), or neroli (*citrus aurantium*) can provide a lighter, fresh touch instead. Fill a glass spray bottle with seven drops of one essential oil and water. Shake well before misting room and pillows. You can also allow the slow release of the fragrance with scented candles or an electric diffuser.

Be sure to capture these fun moments on film and share the photos later. Serve food and a beverage, but keep it simple—your main focus is fun.

> *Laughter is a tranquilizer with no side effects.*
> —*Arnold Glasow (1943–1996)*

Conundrums

Cultivation to the mind is as necessary as food to the body.
—*Marcus Tullius Cicero (106–43 B.C.)*

We all get so involved in the hectic pace of everyday life that we forget how simple pleasures can be. Mental stimulation is as much fun as active play and another way to wake up the whole body.

The infamous *Rubik's Cube* was actually invented by the architect and teacher Erno Rubik in Budapest, Hungary, in the 1970s to help his students recognize the spatial relationships in three dimensions. The same puzzle design was also credited to

Japanese engineer, Terutoshi Ishige. In North America during the 1980 holiday season, this new toy shot to the top of the sales charts.

Today, there are both regional and international competitions where contestants race the clock to restore each side of the cube to a single color. This evening, challenge your mind with this fun, twist-of-the-hand game. It may enthrall you for hours.

For a relaxing afternoon, give one of Billie Holiday's collections a try. I recommend
Body and Soul (Gold CD), a remix version of her slow and rich lyrics.

Treat yourself like a guest in your own home and before you put out the games and puzzles, try a new beverage recipe today: Lebanese white coffee. Paradoxically, it is not a coffee, but an herbal tea made with orange blossom water, which calms the nerves and stimulates digestion after a heavy meal. If serving in the tiny, decorative, Lebanese-style glasses, place a little spoon in each glass prior to pouring the boiling water to avoid the glass from breaking.

Lebanese White Coffee

1 teaspoon of orange blossom water

lemon zest

raw sugar cubes

Heat a saucepan of 1½ cups of water. Once the water starts to simmer, add the orange blossom water until it boils. Remove from heat and serve hot with a lemon zest and sweeten to taste.

To start off this Sunday morning in a leisurely fashion, pick up a sharpened pencil and start a new ritual of fun—crossword puzzles, word search puzzles, or word scramble games. With a cup of hot tea, coffee, or glass of fresh-squeezed orange juice, just let time deliberately slip away.

Afterwards, search the local bookstore for books full of mind play, or download a challenge from the many websites that offer a new puzzle every day.

Pieces and Parts

Jigsaw puzzles originated in the 1760s when European mapmakers pasted maps onto wood and cut them into small pieces designed as an educational tool for children to learn geography.

In two centuries of existence, puzzles have gone through a remarkable transformation, beginning in primary classrooms and ending up on parlor tables around the world as an enjoyable pastime for adults. The full-blown craze hit America in the early 1900s when aficionados could be heard mumbling, "just one more piece" into the wee hours of the night.

With the onset of the Depression, puzzle sales peaked in popularity, reaching an astounding ten million sold per week. During this heyday, drugstores and libraries rented these mind twisters for three to ten cents per day.

1965—Jackson Pollock's painting Convergence *is billed as the world's most difficult jigsaw puzzle, testing hundred of thousands of Americans' mental dexterity.*

On a colder than normal afternoon, spread a five thousand piece jigsaw or three-dimensional puzzle across the dining room table or floor and promise yourself not to get up until it is completed. Add uplifting mood music and a pot of loose leaf white Chinese tea to your party for one. Also known as Mutant White, White Peony tea, and Pai Mu Tan, this tea is only harvested a few days of the year in the Fujian province, making it one of the rarest and most expensive of teas—but you deserve to try this golden beverage with a mellow taste. (Hint: use more tea leaves than you would with black or green.)

Puzzles are a perfect way to de-stress on a steaming hot August day, too. Make the tea iced and you'll have it made in the shade.

The Dirty Dozen Brass Band *by* Medicated Magic *is pure New Orleans with rhythm set by trumpets, piano, and deep-south vocals guaranteed to uplift and mentally stimulate those playing games.*

THE LOST ART OF CARD PLAYING

How to make an Italian forty-card deck: for the game Briscola, remove the Jokers, eights, nines, and tens from a standard fifty-two card deck. To learn how to play Briscola, see page 49 of Hoyle's Rules of Games, *or check the Internet.*

Card games have a history of all their own. With diverse origins stemming from Italy to France, the Orient, and the early days in the United States, each game offers participants a chance to improve their keen sense of observation, memory, and inference.

Invite three to seven of your good friends over to learn to play Euchre. This card game originated with the arrival of the Dutch in Pennsylvania around 1864, which then gave rise to Five Hundred.

I still remember the nights of card playing with my grandparents. Due to their combined and cumulative years of experience—weekly practice sessions with their Bridge club—they were very good. But both had the patience to teach my brother, sister, and me new games every time we visited.

Bridge was developed from the English game Whist around 1742 and is one of the most popular card games in the English-speaking world. It ranks a close second in popularity with the rest of the world.

Being a writer, my family game suggestion is always *Scrabble,* but this year I promised my daughter to teach her the lost card games of Bloody Knuckles, War, and Crazy Eights. These are my childhood card games that I played during long and hot summers in Belleville, Pennsylvania.

With young children who think that they are too old for naps, introduce card games. Teach them how to play Go Fish or Old Maid.

For a new twist on the old-favorite ice cream and soda drink, pull out the punch bowl. Add a liter or two of root beer and five or six scoops of vanilla ice cream. Let the kids serve themselves. Between the card game and their fun-to-drink beverage, you will have them captivated for at least twenty minutes.

> *The game of Cribbage came into existence by way of a lost and older game called Noddy. English poet, Sir John Suckling (1609–1642), is believed to have invented Cribbage by borrowing several features from Noddy. When early colonists brought this peg and card game to the New World, it flourished.*

The last time I was on book tour, I called home to say hello and found that I had interrupted a game of poker (complete with cigars) between my husband and daughter—bubble gum cigars I discovered later to my relief. My husband was also instrumental in introducing my daughter to Cribbage, a game that he had learned from his father, who learned it from his father, and so on.

Life consists not in holding good cards but in playing those you hold well.
—*Arnold Glasow (1943–1996)*

Take your passion to a new level and sign up for the town's card game, chess tournament, or the weekly Bridge games. If your town is lacking in such regular fun, take the initiative to set up the challenge.

SOLITAIRE

The origin of peg solitaire dates back to the 1600s and was reputedly invented out of boredom by a French nobleman imprisoned in the Bastille. The object of the game is for the player to jump the thirty-two wooden pegs with only one remaining in the center hole.

For another twist on this game, pull out a deck of cards for an entertaining game of solitaire. Bring this peacefulness with you to work, too, and play a game after lunch today.

Checkers, first invented in France about nine hundred years ago, was named after the French word for chessboard, eschequier, *since both games use the same platform.*

If social interaction is what your spirit craves, take a portable board game of checkers, Chinese checkers, backgammon, or chess and invite a fellow business associate to join you for some fun at noon. Chinese checkers is great for up to five players. Set up a quick and easy backgammon tournament with best two games out of three, or best three out of five—winner pays for lunch! You'll be amazed at how chess will sharpen your strategic skills. Add a little French flair to your game of chess and say, "*Esche!*" whenever you are about to capture your opponent's king. Who knows? Your passion might spread among others and might be the start of more laughs at your workplace.

> **A mind that is stretched
> to a new idea never returns
> to its original dimension.**
> —*Oliver Wendell Holmes (1841–1935)*

FAMILY IN THE ORCHARD
BY THEO VAN RYSSELBERGHE

CHAPTER EIGHT

It's a Woman Thing

LIKE MINDS AND BODIES UNITE

Play is the exultation of the possible.
—*Martin Buber (1901–1992)*

This is your secret invitation to gather with other like-minded women who play wholeheartedly and without guilt. Find these other women who respect and celebrate their gifts and openly embrace life. When joined with other women for pure fun and lots of laughs, you will see that fun knows no age and that there are no limits nor boundaries on play. This newfound happiness will be achieved through active and creative play together.

It's the friends you can call at 4 A.M. that matter.
—*Marlene Dietrich (1901–1992)*

*Research studies show that high levels of social support
help increase resistance to stress-induced illnesses.*

There used to be only a handful of other women; now there are twenty to thirty in each [mountain bike race] category.
—Chrissy Redden (b. 1966), mountain bike racer, 2000 Olympian, 2001 World Cup Champion

Recruit and organize other like-minded women for simply the single cause of mutual support. Swap baby-sitting, share stories, toys, tools, and laughs along the way, too. Together, set out to make a change for the betterment of all involved. Be each other's creative muse or coach. Be there for each other as often as you can in the physical sense or sometimes only in spirit. Count on your friends for accountability, extra motivation, and their unconditional support.

Play is an activity that makes my friends, family, and me smile.
—Molly Wilson, Joplin, Missouri

If you hesitate to try something new, take a friend along. Convince her it is for her own good, for the good of both of you. With the two of you playing, your fun will be doubled, plus it will be easier to spin yarns about your adventure later from different points of view. Go back to night school together, take a mini-vacation, or sign up for outdoor activities such as horseback-riding, mountain-biking, backpacking, snow camping, or llama-trekking.

1911—Nan Jane Aspinwall, the first woman to make a solo transcontinental horseback ride, crosses the United States in 301 days, covering four thousand five hundred miles.

INVITE MOTHERS AND DAUGHTERS

Once bitten by the play bug, you will be on the lookout for even more fun within your current new love. Now you know that both active and creative play are good for women of all ages, including our daughters. Together, in this new time made, the lines between leader and follower, adult and child blur. Moms will invite daughters and daughters will encourage moms. This Mother's Day, decide to play the way that you have always wanted to do—go off on a scuba-diving cruise, a weekend yoga retreat, or start training for a multiple-event team race—and bring your little girl along (even if she's already taller than you are!).

1908—President Wilson proclaims the second Sunday of May will be a national holiday known as Mother's Day.

Join your daughter in her sport to find the confidence to say, "Yes," to an activity new to you. Recently, I accompanied my daughter on a horseback-riding charity event. In our household, she is the experienced equestrian rider, having ridden for six years, whereas

I have been on a horse six times in my life. Her sense of confidence, riding skills, and natural ability put me at ease for the five-mile ride. Without her coaching and presence, I would have been nervous, which the horse would have sensed and could have made for a long ride.

WOMEN'S NIGHT OUT

Declare any night "Women's Night Out," but hit the gym to try a new water yoga class, swim laps, play water polo, or play pool basketball with friends. Sign up for an evening class or try out for a team. Meet for a chess tournament, a rough-and-tumble soccer game, or a sunset hike to the top of a local mountain. Any way you book it, simply enjoy this time made to develop interests and deepen friendships.

THE WORKING DILEMMA

Work and play do mix. Play can actually open the brain to new ideas and solutions. Schedule it and plan for your time in the pool, at the gym, or just being outside at some point of the work day. Respect this time as if it is a meeting with a very important client, and it is—you.

When I worked in advertising, 90 percent of the time, others (clients, vendors, and employees) commanded my time, yet I still made space in my day for play. Some weeks, it had to be before or after work. I lived about thirty miles from my office, so with a little ingenious planning and the extra assistance of my husband with my daughter, I departed (early) for work by bike. The day before my ride, I would leave work clothes, a suit and heels, at my office so I would able to shower and change at the local gym, which was walking distance from my agency. It was a wondrous way to begin any week or any day.

Other times, I relied heavily on my energetic art director, Julie, to get me to the gym at noon. During the work week, count on your active business associates to motivate you.

CHERISHED GEMS

If you are searching for another source of inspiration, need instruction, or are stuck on the intermediate level, call upon an enthused friend. Under her protective wing this is where your dreams can be tried without judgment, and where learning and stumbling will be unconditionally supported. Use this safe haven as a stepping-stone to perfect a craft, art, or sporting skill.

Keep these cherished gems in your life close by—those friends who inspire you to dream big and also reach your aspirations.

Sweet peas, known for their fragrant bouquet, are definitely a great "thank you"
gift for any muse in your life. Take a bunch to her today.

ROLE MODELS

We owe it to the women of the future to encourage young girls to express themselves through sports. Sports are not just a display of athletic power; they are a tool to help develop self-esteem and a healthy image.

—Peggy Fleming (b.1948), 1968 Olympic Gold Medallist Figure Skating Champion, three-time World Champion

According to the 2000 census numbers, there are almost twenty million girls in the United States between the ages of ten and nineteen. These young women can be our next leaders, chemists, engineers, or professional athletes, and more importantly, the mentors and mothers of the next generation. Be an example to your daughter, your neighbor's daughter, nieces, and especially little girls who need to see women who are happy in their own skin. Show them what your body and mind can do.

Girls need to hear it is OK to play basketball or any other boy's sport and that they can be feminine at the same time.

—Sheryl Swoopes (b. 1971), basketball player, 1996 Olympic Gold, 1995–96 member of the U.S. National Team with a historic 52-0 record

Music is an intergenerational language. Introduce the younger set to a few of your favorite female vocalists: Anita Baker, the Supremes, Bonnie Raitt, Joni Mitchell, Stevie Nicks, or Melissa Etheridge. In return, they will share their take on the latest releases by Sheryl Crow, Nelly Furtado, the Dixie Chicks, Erykah Badu, or Macy Gray.

Help cultivate the future of strong-minded, strong-bodied women by being such a role model. Start a monthly mother-daughter weekend outing and go outside to play. It does not have to be a hike to the top of Mt. Everest—your adventure could be over the next knoll across the valley.

Rotate activities and locations to find new fun. Laughter is contagious and necessary when attempting new activities, so include it in your outing. In this reserved time, add brand new, outdoor activities. Try bouldering, fishing, or paddling. When you do make this step, you will be smiling from within and will be free in spirit and body.

Go play and invite the younger generation to join you.

***Athletics are the best antidote for the
poison of premature love affairs.***

—*May Sutton (1886–1975), first American woman to win Wimbledon, won in 1905*

INFLUENCE THE FUTURE

1972—Title IX signed into law June 23 states:"No person in the United States shall, on the basis of sex, be excluded from participation in, be denied the benefits of, or be subjected to discrimination under any education program or activity receiving federal financial assistance."

For women born before or near the passing of Title IX, the notion of following her sport as a means of earning a livelihood was a dead end street. However, this legislation launched a whole new playing field for our daughters, and even for their moms who never had a chance to play as little girls, opportunities are now wide open.

> ***Before Title IX there was no reason to swim beyond high school…because of scholarships [today] there are many older female swimmers still competing. Now we can become professionals and make a living.***
> —*Jenny Thompson (b. 1973), swimmer, five-time Olympic Gold, five-time World Champion, eighteen-time U.S. National Champion*

The difference between the younger generation who plays sports as naturally as they breathe, and their mothers who grew up being told, "No, it's not ladylike," is their increasing number of opportunities and role models. Female athletes are now household names, and the reality of being able to make a career of play is happening.

At fifteen, Tara Lipinski was the youngest female ever to win the Ladies' U.S. National Figure Skating and World Championship titles. She won the gold at the 1998 Olympics.

Today, when a little girl says she wants to grow up to be a professional ice hockey player or softball player, her dream has roots. Her goal has the power and the possibility of coming true. Encourage her to strive for her dream by accomplishing yours.

Never doubt that you can change history. You already have.
——*Marge Piercy (b. 1936)*

SUPPORTIVE ENVIRONMENTS
Hope springs exulting on triumphant wing.
——*Robert Burns (1759–1796)*

Find environments that will nurture your natural abilities. I find comfort and peaceful solitude writing in bookstores, libraries, and colleges. These places are plentiful sources of knowledge and kind-hearted people, a natural location for me to be inspired to write my best.

Be friendly to the people who supply your toys or tools. They may introduce you to others who have similar interests or can tell you if a related clinic is being held in your city.

The first thing that education teaches you is to walk alone.
—*Alfred Aloysius Horn (1854–1927)*

Find your motivation back in the classroom. Review the course catalog from your local college to see what will engage your mind. How about conversational Italian, or beginning ceramics, or African dance?

If the closest college makes for a long commute, try the courses available on the Internet. Search the at-a-distance learning centers and universities for topics of interest to you.

I've always believed that one woman's success can only help another woman's success.
—*Gloria Vanderbilt (b. 1924)*

GROUP THERAPY
The only way to have a friend is to be one.
—*Ralph Waldo Emerson (1803–1882)*

Writers form groups, quilters gather to create, and golf fanatics will always be looking for a foursome. There is power in knowing others who experience your same passion. Find these people. Your new friends will help to ignite your hidden talents and vice versa. These kindred souls are worth the search. Invite them into your life, along with their knowledge, skill, and enthusiasm, and fun will follow them in the door, too.

TEAM SPORTS, TEAM RACES
The three-day, two-night Avon Breast Cancer walk from San Jose to San Francisco was one of the toughest things that I ever did—but with the goal of finding a cure for this terrible disease and my friends alongside me—it was worth all of every mile and blister.
—*Susan Hilton, Coto de Caza, California*

Apply the axiom "the more the merrier." Those who have experienced endurance races, marathon walks, and other mind-, body-, and spirit-challenging opportunities can attest to this truth. The dynamics of a group will help you achieve your goal, which may appear unattainable on your own.

Use the momentum of the group to bring out your best, especially when attempting the unknown—an ingredient all forms of true adventure must hold. Learn and inspire each other, too. Best of all, you will not be traveling alone. So, whether you sign up for a week-long arts and crafts retreat, an ultramarathon, or simply want to take a snorkeling cruise, invite a friend or two, or three.

Together, anticipate and prepare for the big event. If the choice activity requires a basic level of fitness, everyone can set off for the gym or trails twice a week on the quest for better health and good times with friends.

Lavender Infused Bath: After your active bout with friends, fill the tub with warm water and add five to seven drops of essential oil of lavender (lavandula angustifolia). Light a lavender-scented candle and reach for the bar of old-fashioned milled lavender soap. Indulge yourself in this relaxing, fragrant ambience. Your nighttime sleep should be quite sound tonight.

On days when you do not feel like getting out the door, you will have your playing buddies to rely on. Enlist your friends to help you win your personal battle when you start to hesitate about what is important today—working, cleaning, or playing.

The weeks spent together will bond your group in a new way, promising memories that will last a lifetime and encouraging additional outings after this one.

Play can be an activity that one chooses to do alone or with others that brings enjoyment and promotes a sense of well-being.
—Linda McHenry, Topeka, Kansas

CREATIVE CELEBRATIONS
Exchange is creation.
—*Muriel Rukeyser (1931–1980)*

Invite a few creative friends over for an inspirational dinner. Replace the old tablecloth and centerpiece with butcher paper and a jar of crayons. Have others bring colored pencils, paints, charcoal, and pastels—along with a dish to share. Eat, but focus on making your marks for the world to see. Draw big and definitely do not stay inside the lines. Be brave. Paint in loud colors. Leave your masterpiece on the table or hang it up until the next celebration of creating occurs.

ART PARTIES
There are two ways of spreading the light: be the
candle or the mirror that reflects it.
—*Edith Wharton (1862–1937)*

As your talent emerges, use your home's hallway as a museum corridor. Beneath each masterpiece, put a card with its title: "Moments in Nature" ("Untitled" will work, too), your name, and the date. As your portfolio becomes larger and your art covers other walls in your house, send out invitations and host a party for art lovers—your friends who will in turn invite you to their art shows. Make these gatherings a circle of unconditional support.

ANNUAL GALAS

Dig through your closet and drawers for items no longer your style. Invite a few friends over and ask them to bring clothes that they have not worn in two decades or two years. Strictly for the fun of it, try on each other's clothes. What once complimented you may look fabulous on your next-door-neighbor. Trade it to her for something that she has lost her love for.

For the cost of a few appetizers, beverages, and a roll of film full of hilarious memories, you and your friends will have a rollicking fun time and perhaps end up with a new outfit. End the fashion show with a trip to the local charity to donate the remaining items. This "look good, feel good" event could become an annual celebration of fun among friends.

Stay is a charming word in a friend's vocabulary.
—*Louisa May Alcott (1832–1881)*

LIKE MINDS AND BODIES UNITE

I grew up a tomboy, much to the chagrin of my parents, and at the time, I secretly appreciated yet resented the label. I did not know that you could be both feminine and athletic.

As an adult, not much has changed—except now I call myself an athlete. I am a mountain biker, not a woman on a bike; I am a skier, not a woman on skis, and that is the way it should be. It has taken society—and women in particular, including myself—a long time to see women this way. Today's younger generation is being raised as athletes, both male and female, and as a result, these like minds and bodies are united through sports.

> *I was not doing any sport until I met my husband,*
> *who taught me all of it. I was then in my thirties.*
> —Chantal Kane, Paris, France

The fact is that it was my male friends who repeatedly showed me the importance of keeping play in my life. They still play as adults—whether they are working husbands, single parents, or career men. It does not matter if I am cycling with a $350-an-hour tax attorney, the president of a mortgage company, or an engineer; they keep laughter, bad jokes, and of course, fun, in this time. They still find the time to read, to go on adventures to appreciate the arts, or to create pasta from scratch.

I think we, as women, could stand to learn from them. I know I did.

SECOND CAREERS

My writer friend, Sam, has started his second career after forty years in the banking industry. He found his true love, writing, and has published five mystery books in the last five years. An inspiration to all who know him, Sam shows us that it is never too late to begin to play.

DETERMINATION

Tom, my biking friend from Vermont, arrived in Santa Barbara, California, fresh and ready to ride some miles outdoors. He reported that his training for this century ride consisted of listening to the band U2 repeatedly while riding his wind trainer in his cold basement, winter night after winter night.

In spite of a threatening snowstorm at the start, severe coastal winds, the undulating hill playing host to numerous distracting wineries, and the notorious Chalk Hill, we, including "Basement Boy Tom," finished the century in good form and time.

A friend is someone who understands
your past, believes in your
future, and accepts you today
just the way you are.
—*Proverbs 17:17*

Friends like this are hard to find, but find them you must.

PLAY TODAY

Start playing today because someone or something will always need your attention. Start playing today no matter what shape or size your body. It is through playing that you will be in the body you love. The best news is that the more you play, the prouder you will be of the results.

Call a friend. Now. Trust me on this matter. Today is a beautiful day to go play.

Seek not outside yourself, heaven is within.
—Mary Lou Cook (b. 1918)

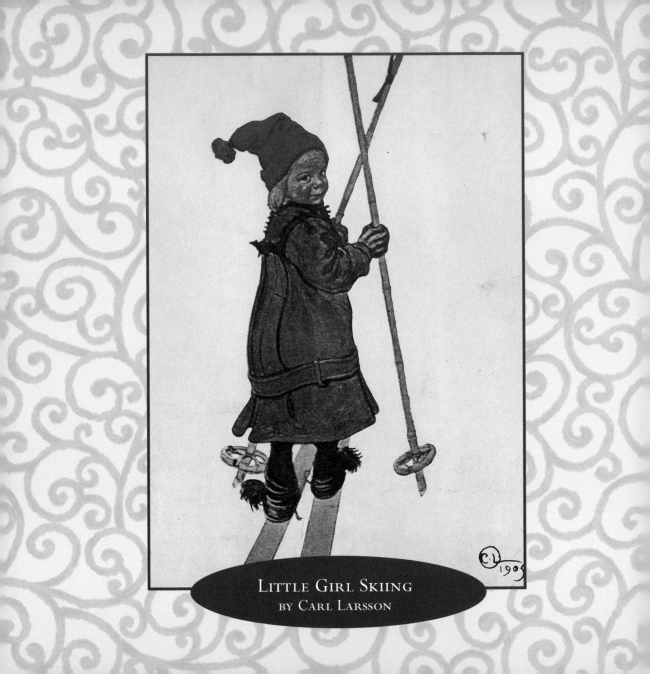

LITTLE GIRL SKIING
BY CARL LARSSON

CHAPTER NINE

Age is Irrelevant

GO PLAY!

What lies behind us and what lies before us are tiny matters compared to what lies within us.
—Ralph Waldo Emerson (1803–1882)

Based on his Pulitzer Prize-winning series for the *Chicago Tribune*, science writer Ronald Kotulak's new book supports the theory that the brain craves positive training, education, and experience throughout life. In *Inside the Brain: Revolutionary Discoveries of How the Mind Works*, he claims, "The brain's plasticity factor allows new learning and relearning to take place at any age."

Kotulak also writes that the more synapses, or connections, one has between brain cells, the more resistant they are to the effects of Alzheimer's.

Contrary to conventional wisdom, people do not lose a massive number of brain cells as they age; experts are finding that the brain's functions simply get rusty with disuse. Intellectual decline varies widely, but is mainly dependent on how much mental fire is kept ablaze.

"There isn't much difference between a twenty-five-year-old brain and a seventy-five-year-old brain," says Monte Buchsbaum, director of the Neuroscience Laboratory at Mount Sinai School of Medicine in New York City.

Visit your local health food store to learn more about herbs and vitamins that boost mental alertness. Ask about gingko biloba, ginseng, spirulina, and soy-based drinks.

Tropical Treat

1 mango
1 banana
1 cup of sweetened coconut milk
1 cup of soy milk
3-5 ice cubes

Fill the blender with the fruit, pour in coconut milk and soy milk and top with ice cubes. Blend thoroughly and garnish with an orange slice. Freeze the leftover mixture to eat as a popsicle later.

Further medical findings now show that memory loss can be delayed or even restored. Aerobic activity, resistance training, and other exercises improve overall health, which has a beneficial filtering effect for all mental health functions. More specifically, exercise fights stress and depression that has been proven to interfere with memory.

POWERFUL BODY, POWERFUL MIND

Dispense the stimulating properties of the essential oil of thyme (thymus vulgaris) via water or steam distillation or visit a local nursery to pick up a potted plant for your creative sanctuary. Thyme blends well with bergamot (citrus bergamia).

What matters most is that we learn from living.
—Doris Lessing (b. 1919)

The power that comes from moving our bodies and minds has a cumulative effect, and over the years and decades, continues to grow stronger. No matter at what age you begin or return to playing, from the very first day, this new active time in your days will benefit you for the rest of your life. No one can take that away from you. This strength stays with you in the form of muscle and memory, the deep satisfaction of having the experience, and the knowledge that you know you can do it again. The adage, "You never forget how to ride a bike," reiterates this valid point completely.

We don't stop playing because we grow old, we grow old because we stop playing.
—George Bernard Shaw (1856–1950)

Play gives the confidence to do, to be, and above all else, to shine. Believe in yourself. Age is irrelevant on your quest for fun. Set an example of what is to be a woman of your age and stature. Remember, it is just eight supermodels against the rest of us.

I have no regrets. I wouldn't have lived my life the way I did if I
were going to worry about what people were going to say.
—*Ingrid Bergman (1915–1982)*

Take to trekking distant lands where few speak your language. Grow a fabulous garden of kitchen herbs and experiment with new applications for each. Start your art career at any age or compile your first chapbook of poetry. If the sky has always attracted you, learn to pilot a plane or skydive.

Show the naysayers that there is no end to what you can do. Be a role model to the younger generation, and show the little girls of the world where your strong and steady feet have taken you. Use your hands to create, design, and play. Life is too precious just to watch it go by. Follow your heart. Listen to the friendly voice inside your head and tell the negative one to take a hike, alone.

As you grow older, you'll find the only things you
regret are the things you didn't do.
—*Zachary Scott (1914–1965)*

Create your own fortitude by reaching for your dreams and making them a long list in your life's accomplishments. Display your accomplishments: your ribbons, trophies, and medals. Keep your T-shirts earned from walking or running a 5K. Make a clipping book of your awards, newspaper articles, photos, certificates, or letters of recognition. Embrace the passing years as an integral part of what makes you who you are. Be on your way to establishing a life full of adventures—do not let a number stand in your way.

The great thing about getting older is that
you don't lose all the other ages you've been.
—*Madeline L'Engle (b. 1918)*

GROW GRACEFULLY
I would like to grow very old as slowly as possible.
—*Irene Mayer Selznick (1907–1990)*

View and accept aging, not as growing old, but growing gracefully. With every passing day, expand yourself, your knowledge, and your hunger for life. Learning is the secret of a happy life, a never-ending process that keeps the mind, body, and spirit young at heart.

If we don't change, we don't grow. If we don't grow, we aren't really living.
—*Gail Sheehy (b. 1937)*

Listen to the music selection entitled Euphoria *and begin to explore your options for active and creative play. Sit back, close your eyes, and start on your journey of self-fulfillment.*

Ancoro imparo. (Latin for "I am still learning.")
—Michelangelo in his eighty-seventh year (1475–1564)

The scent of essential oil of rose (rosa centifolia)
is an excellent way to begin
each day. Try scented body powder, line your
clothes drawers and closet with
perfumed linen paper, or place a dozen fragrant buds in your bedroom.

BEGINNER'S MIND

No one grows old by living—only by losing interest in living.
—Marie Beynon Ray (1890–1969)

1959—Choreographer and modern dance pioneer Martha Graham,
sixty-five, wins the ninth annual Capezio Award.

At any given point in our lives, depending on how we choose to spend our days, we are either growing or dying. As a child, we grow in great leaps and bounds, both physically and mentally, learning, seeking out the new, and exploring with an open mind. The Japanese have a term for this curiosity; they call it "beginner's mind."

As adults, we continue to grow, but become focused in our life. We become "experts" in our defined area. In our haste, we neglect to note that change and growth must come from inside, and this transformation requires continual action.

Pick a form of play completely new to you and try it. Try your hand at calligraphy, weaving, or basketry. Learn to play chess, backgammon, or Bridge. Plan a trip to the coast to play beach volleyball with friends and family or go calming along the shore. Go inside to find what your spirit desires and prepare to step outside your comfort zone.

> **Nothing is worth more than this day.**
> —*Johann Wolfgang Goethe (1749–1832)*

STATE OF MIND

This weekend, observe the neighborhood golf course, baseball field, basketball, or tennis courts, or simply check the runners or cyclists along the side of the road. Lots of people are out there moving—no matter what size or age—and having fun while doing it. This time set aside is not a requirement; play is something to do for fun and is even better with a group of friends. Do not let age stop you. If anything, take each passing year as an opportunity to chalk up another success and look forward to the new 365 days to gain even more from life.

2002—Paula Newby-Fraser at thirty-nine becomes the oldest person ever to win an Ironman
Triathlon at her twenty-third competition on Fukue Island, Japan.
She has more Ironman titles than anyone in the world.

Make the most of life's journey and do not let the word "age" stop you—for it is through our play that learning can continue. Many women have surrendered to the excuse, "I am too old for that."

Says who?

Each of us still holds inside ourselves the enthusiasm of a young girl poised to tackle whatever challenge stands before her. Perhaps we have listened to others for too many years and now do not think we can. Maybe our busy lives did not allow us to play as often as we would have liked when we were younger and we fear we cannot remember how to get started.

Mountain climbing pioneer Annie Smith Peck scaled the highest summits of
the world up until her death at age eighty-five in 1935.

My artist friend Susie, from Pittsburgh, Pennsylvania, talks about taking ballet classes, but thinks that she is crazy to start at her age. I wholeheartedly disagree and encourage her to sign up every time I speak to her. Do not let your age be a deterrent in your pursuit of happiness. I am going to enroll in a martial arts class again at the age of thirty-nine. It has been four years since I won second place at a jujitsu tournament, and I am hungry to learn more and move up another belt.

> *How old would you be if you didn't know how old you are?*
> —*Satchel Paige (1906–1982)*

BRAZEN WOMEN

All it takes is the audacity to say, "I can do it," and then the tenacity to follow through with your desire. Gatekeepers, doubting Toms, and other misinformed people who believe older women cannot and should not be seen playing will tell you so. It simply goes against logic in their own minds, but who are they to say who gets to play and who does not? The only person who truly knows what works for you is you.

> *Old age is no place for sissies.*
> —*Bette Davis (1908–1989)*

Listen to your inner voice. Go play with your paints by the river. Take the dog for a run. Whatever you decide to do, be sure to wear a bright color so the world will see an older woman enjoying herself at play.

At first people refuse to believe that a strange new thing can be done, then they begin to hope it can be done, then they see it can be done—then it is done and all the world wonders why it was not done centuries ago.
—Frances Hodgson Burnett (1907–1954)

Pick up a Ball

I never guessed that I'd still be racing at this point. Cross-country is an endurance sport, and getting older doesn't take you out of the running. It's hard not to think about Athens in 2004.
—Alison Sydor at 35, cross-country mountain bike racer, three-time World Champion, three-time World Cup Overall Winner, two-time Olympian

Thirty-four-year-old Kari Blinn, a native Californian, tried out for the New England Storm and was named the team's quarterback. During the day, she is a senior consultant for colleges and universities.

Working mom Carla O'Neil, originally from Sumter, South Carolina, has taken up gymnastics at the age of thirty-nine without anyone's permission.

Mary Miller Giovanetti from Honesdale, Pennsylvania, has studied yoga for more than thirty years and added tai chi in the last seven years.

According to Runner's World, *the ancient art of tai chi has been shown to reduce blood pressure and ease arthritis symptoms. In studies, sixty-five- to ninety-six-year-olds who took a tai chi class twice a week saw a 70 percent improvement in their abilities to lift and bend.*

We all have the ability to master a sport. The only difference is that some women play more. Never be too busy to address your passion. Look at the entire week to determine what you can let go, what can be combined, or what to delegate or cancel—this is where an extra hour or two can be found.

Do it for your physical and mental health. You (and everyone around you) will be glad that you took the time.

> *I am not afraid of storms for I am learning how to sail my ship.*
> —Louisa May Alcott (1832–1888)

In the March 2001 issue of Prevention *magazine, writer Michele Stanten suggests that one of the keys to making exercise a habit is to do something you enjoy.*

Take the time to create fun in your life today. Play is what gives your life sparkle, your body extra energy, and your mind a clearer perspective on what is important in life and what is insignificant. You can do whatever you put your mind to.

Paul Konstanty, exercise therapist with the Physical Rehabilitation Network in San Diego, California, says, "Fitness doesn't have to be confined within four walls of a gym. There are all kinds of activities that you can do and sports that you can play to have fun and keep fit."

PICK UP A BRUSH

Alma Thomas (American abstract artist 1891–1978) first dreamed of becoming a bridge architect, but prepared for a career as a teacher. After thirty-five years of teaching at Shaw Junior High School in Washington, D.C., the sixty-nine-year-old earned the prestigious honor of being the first African-American woman to have a solo exhibition at New York City's Whitney Museum of American Art in 1972.

Judie Day built a pottery studio to celebrate her fiftieth birthday. A year later, she opened Laloba Ranch to the public for classes. Sandy Schneider, a creative spirit who has been singing all of her life, left a teaching job at age fifty-one to be a writer. At thirty-three, Josephine Murphy blows glass for relaxation from working on her master's degree.

What do these women all have in common? Each has a passion for living. They take the time to do what fills them up emotionally, spiritually, physically, and mentally.

Invite your creative muse to join you—no matter what stage of life you are living. You are a sum of your thoughts, experiences, actions, and dreams. Put this good life to use. Creativity has no boundaries, no limitations; anyone can create, invent, and produce.

What is stopping you from playing in your new art? Who says you cannot start your art career at fifty-seven? Go visit an art store today or at least get online and explore art supply sources.

Why not take piano lessons at sixty-two? Check the phone book for a music teacher or call the local schools for a referral.

*2002—The Hardwood Museum of Art in Taos, New Mexico, opens the first
abstract exhibit by artist Agnes Martin. She is ninety years old.*

How many books do you still want to read in this lifetime? Make that list of books
to read. Stuck? Ask a librarian or a bibliophile to get you started.

> **The one thing I regret is that
> I will never have time to read all the books I want to read.**
> —*Francoise Sagan (b. 1935)*

How many books do you have in you to write?
Start those idea files and watch the pages come
together. Buy a blank journal and write poetry.

If you cannot remember the last time you
picked up a paintbrush, be gentle on yourself in
terms of your expectations. Paint, but expect
the result of a kindergartner. We are all creative
beings, artists in the rough. All that is needed is
practice. The more time spent exploring a passion,
inevitably the more proficient your skills will
become.

The life you have led doesn't need to be the only life you have.
—Anna Quindlen (b. 1953)

Now is the time to release your creative self. Do not count the years left—only look forward to each day as it comes. Think of all your experiences from which to layer, develop, and design your art. Let your imagination come up with a new board game, or use your artistic skills to sketch a new design to be patented for the world's benefit.

What are you going to do first?

Play is the highest form of research.
—Albert Einstein (1879–1955)

Patent Your Ideas: For more information, call 800-786-9199, visit www.uspto.gov, or write to General Information Services Division, U.S. Patent and Trademark Office, Crystal Plaza 3, Room 2C02, Washington, D.C. 20231.

LIFE'S WAKE-UP CALLS

I've said it many times. Cancer has made me a better athlete and it has made me a better person.
—Lance Armstrong (b. 1972), four-time winner of the Tour de France

Numerous stories from strong-willed people tell of how their disease transformed them for the better. Without their illness, they would not have become the person they are today. As severe as it sounds, there is truth in their words. Olympian Gold runner Gail Devers lives with Graves Disease. Others fight cancer, multiple sclerosis, and leukemia. These individuals have faced death or stepped back from the brink to see how truly brilliant each day can be.

> *I never looked at asthma, my condition, as being a handicap. My attitude*
> *was to beat asthma. I wasn't going to allow asthma to get the best of me.*
> —*Jackie Joyner-Kersee (b. 1962), three-time Olympic Gold,*
> *world record holder for the heptathalon since 1986*

Consider the accident, the illness, the turn of events beyond your control a "wake-up call" to start living life. See obstacles as challenges and rise not only to meet, but also to conquer them.

About ten years ago I became too focused on work and neglected my health. My "wake-up call" came in a wave of three accidents. First, I tore my anterior cruciate ligament and fractured my tibia while skiing. The second accident came the following winter when I reinjured the same knee, spraining the meniscus. A year later, I fractured two ribs during a bicycle collision with a moving car.

Thirty-five is when you finally get your head
together and your body starts falling apart.
—Caryn Leschen (b. 1954)

However, after each setback, I came back. After reconstructive knee surgery and three months of physical therapy, and another round of physical therapy the following year with the second knee injury—I skied again. After the ribs healed, I biked again. Today, I am still playing—biking until the snow falls and skiing as many as possible of the more than one hundred twenty days of winter.

NEVER TOO LATE

Medical findings prove that by the age of sixty-five our bodies can lose 30 to 40 percent of the ability to efficiently use oxygen. Regular aerobic exercise can help prevent this decline.

Marilyn Albert, a Harvard University neurologist and director of gerontology at Massachusetts General Hospital, studied more than one thousand people between the ages of seventy to eighty. The study revealed several factors in holding onto both physical and mental capacities: 1) continuing education, which appears to increase the number and strength of synaptic connections; 2) strenuous activity, improving the blood flow to the brain and strengthening the lungs, guaranteeing blood is adequately oxygenated; and 3) the feeling that what they do makes a difference.

Claim a passion, make it your own, something that can live with you all your days. Over the years, your sport or hobby will make you stronger, more determined, and focused. It will carry you through tough times.

As you play, whatever problems weigh heavily upon your shoulders will drift away with the passing of minutes. You will feel relieved afterwards —no matter how bad the painting or how brief the bike ride might have been. Any time spent in play will give you courage, energy, and most importantly, a positive attitude for living.

Researchers at Duke University reported that seniors who undertook a four-month exercise program showed significant improvement in memory and other cognitive functions.

And in the end it's not the years in your life that count. It's the life in your years.
—*Abraham Lincoln (1809–1865)*

Amaze Yourself

1993—Lynn Hill (b. 1961) stuns the rock-climbing world by "freeing the Nose"—becoming the first person to climb Yosemite's El Capitan unaided. She said, "A big part of that climb was to make a statement that a woman can do something that is going to blow people's mind about what's possible." Hill used free-climbing techniques with only her footwork, skill, and physical strength to pull herself up the unyielding three thousand-foot rock wall.

My sister met an older woman the other day while walking her dog in Long Beach, California. The woman, who looked about sixty, was on her way to her tai chi class. She proudly told my sister she was eighty and said she started taking the class five years ago when she could barely get out of bed or through the day due to her arthritis.

> *Play to me is doing something physical that*
> *makes me feel young, free, and strong.*
> —*Dawn Alper, Dorer, New Jersey*

Judy Clemens, born in 1944 in Bell, California, did not start to play racquetball until 1980. Five years later, she won the California Championship. Currently, she organizes mountain bike rides for an Orange County group and rides five times a week. During the summer, she swims 1,500 meters twice a week.

What a difference a "can do" attitude makes.

EXPRESS YOURSELF

Even though Italian artist, professional painter, and engraver Elisabetta Sirani (1638–1665) learned to paint in her father's studio, he opposed her pursuing such a career. In her short life, Sirani completed an estimated 170 paintings, fourteen etchings, and a number of drawings. In 1994, she became the first female artist to have her work depicted on a postage stamp with more than 1.1 billion of the Virgin and Child stamp circulated.

Draw inspiration from those who created during their lifetime and let their ingenuity fill your spirit. Embrace the days and years to come as your time to discover something new. Your poems, books, sport records, photography, paintings, or music will speak to the future.

At the age of thirty-six, American Impressionist painter Lilla Cabot Perry (1848–1933) began to train professionally in Giverny where Claude Monet lived and painted. She brought along her paints, her husband, and three daughters. Over the next forty-nine years, she exhibited regularly in Europe and America, received many portrait commissions, and supported her family with the money she made from her talent.

You are never too old to play. Follow your dream even if it is a wish left over from childhood. Amaze your friends, but more importantly, amaze yourself. You have the power. Do not wait another day to start your search for fun. The tomorrows that you keep promising yourself will never come if you keep making up excuses why you cannot do it today.

My own experience has taught me this: if you wait for the perfect moment when all is safe and assured it may never arrive. Mountains will not be climbed, races won, or lasting happiness achieved.
—*Maurice Chevalier (1888–1972)*

BOATING ON THE SEINE
by Pierre Auguste Renoir

CHAPTER TEN

Let's Go

FIELD DAYS AND ROAD TRIPS

Through travel, I first became aware of the outside world; it was through travel that I found my own introspective way into becoming a part of it.
—Eudora Welty (1909–2001)

Women spend enormous amounts of energy and time making sure everyone else is happy—why not spend a little of that caring energy on you? This year decide to spend some quality time regularly with just you to become your own best friend.

Go to your favorite teahouse or coffee shop and treat yourself. Eat slowly and taste each morsel. Put aside a Saturday afternoon to go see a new photography installation at a gallery or attend a folk music concert. If you feel inspired to communicate, introduce yourself to the other like-minded souls who will be all around you.

Spend time alone at home engrossed in your new hobby of scrapbooking or outside in your garden. Do not wait until the kids are grown to spend time with this new friend. Reserve a date with a very special person this weekend who may need some extra attention—you and yourself should become best friends.

In 1699, at the age of fifty-two, German artist Maria Sibylla Merian sold a collection of her paintings and insect specimens in order to finance a trip to the far-flung Dutch colony of Surinam in northern South America. Her intent was to see her art subjects—the land's insects and flora—in person and then paint them.

Thanks to the Interstate Highway System, it is now possible to travel across the country from coast to coast without seeing anything.
—Charles Kuralt (1934–1997)

Get off the usual paths and see the intriguing and the stimulating to challenge both your mind and body. Rely on the newness of your sport, art, or hobby to add the element of excitement to your vacations. Dream up those trips that will truly awaken your spirit, and then go. Be open to all of the possibilities for development, expansion, and awareness.

My favorite thing is to go where I've never been.
—Diane Arbus (1923–1971)

Take to the trail, try any path, and see where it goes. Let curiosity be your guide and allow many hours for exploration. Go around the bend, over the hill, climb above the fog.

You must learn day by day, year by year, to broaden your horizon. The more things you love, the more you are interested in, the more you enjoy, the more you are indignant about, the more you have left when anything happens.
——Muriel Rukeyser (1913–1980)

We travel, some of us forever, to seek other states, other lives, other souls.
—Anaïs Nin (1903–1977)

Use your active or creative play as a new mode of transportation to explore.

The Dipsea, a 7.1-mile trail from Mill Valley to Stinson Beach, California, begins with a staggered start, 676 steps, bushes, rocks, and roots, and no mandated course—you can take short cuts (mostly vertical) if you want to. The annual June race is limited to one thousand five hundred participants and fills up quickly with more than double the number applying, but you can make the cut. The top six hundred to seven hundred from the previous year are a shoo-in, another five hundred applicants are accepted on a first-come, first-served basis via mail, then a silent auction (actually a bribe—applicants send checks in excess of the entry fee), and finally a lottery drawing fill up the remaining spaces. Get your application in early: (413) 331-3550.

Life Lessons

I ran and ran every day and I acquired this sense of determination, this sense of spirit that I would never, never give up, no matter what else happened.
—*Wilma Rudolph (1940–1994), three-time Gold Olympian*

Powerful attributes such as dedication, patience, and discipline are acquired when many hours are spent in a mind-expanding passion or a body-stretching capacity. Mastering a sport, becoming efficient in a craft or knowledgeable about a hobby can also teach those willing to learn much about life.

In your art or playing sports, you will know the importance of maintaining tools and toys. You will understand how to trust your abilities and intuition, and you'll discover how easy it becomes to communicate your enthusiasm about your new passion to others.

Your interest may also teach you the geography of the United States or foreign countries.

Your new sport can show you the importance of staying in shape year-round. Through cross-training, you may find a second love and add new activities to help your strength, endurance, and balance.

Mastery of a sport or hobby comes after many years of letting it live within your life. This sense of freedom is overwhelming; it is here and now that you are one with your passion, moving effortlessly. Your quest can take you on a life-long adventure. When you look back ten, twenty, thirty years from now, you will not believe the distance you have traveled.

I have been an alpine skier for twenty-three years. This is where I have found my peace. With active and creative play in your days, you will learn how deep life can truly be.

NATURE'S INVITATION

1859—New York City's Central Park opens to the public, offering an Eden with 843 acres of greenery. Cherry trees, wisteria pergola, English gardens, and fountains satisfy the city-dwellers' and tourists' desires to be in nature.

In all things of nature there is something of the marvelous.
—Aristotle (384–322 B.C.)

The four seasons were designed for us to explore the newness of the turning days and the potential of playing. To be alone in nature often offers the spirit peace and life balance. This type of quiet satisfaction can only be found in the wilderness because nature has a way of silencing a chattering mind.

Take advantage of this free invitation to go see the alpine flowers blossom, hike and collect a kaleidoscope of fallen autumn leaves, or witness the change in color of the churning winter waves. Let the waterways of the earth take you to a new destination on the map and within yourself. Book an island vacation and learn how to navigate its clear aquamarine waters in the boat of your choice.

Aromatherapy Tip: Peppermint oil (mentha piperata) can help to alleviate symptoms of sea and travel sickness. Splash a handkerchief with a few drops and inhale whenever you need the relief.

This year make a list of national parks to explore. Put up a topographic map of your state and mark trails to hike, snowshoe, or cross-country ski. As the wind dances through the thick green boughs of the blue spruce, skips across the bare branches of the cottonwoods and through the white Aspen stand, decide it still is not too late to explore. Begin your adventure in nature this weekend no matter what the calendar says.

I always wear slacks because of the brambles and maybe the snakes.
—Katharine Hepburn (b. 1907)

In the winter months when the crackle of the wind-swept snow breaks beneath your feet, the singular calling of a magpie or some other hearty feathered soul who chose to remain behind in this winter wonderland makes everything right in the world. Listen for nature's music year-round; it will do your spirit good to hear it regularly.

There is no other door to knowledge than the door Nature opens; and there is no other truth except the truth we discover in Nature.
—Luther Burbank (1849–1926)

FIELD DAYS

Trip Tip: Bird walks invite you to meet your feathered friends indigenous to the area while getting in a hike. Check with the closest state park for regular tours. (Do not forget your binoculars.)

Your field days can be an hour-long or a full-day adventure. Let your zeal for creating fresh, culinary delights lead to the mountains to pick blueberries or hunt for mushrooms deep in the forest. Find new recipes and then set out to unearth the ingredients.

Every autumn, apple-picking and apple pie-eating are big business for the small town of Julian, California. Make your annual pilgrimage to pick apples or even pumpkins, and sample fresh-squeezed cider and hot baked pies in this tiny town in San Diego County.

Take to the back roads to see the rolling mountainsides of the Northeast change into a colorful weave of orange, red, and golden hues and to find a farm offering pumpkins for sale. They might offer hayrides, too. Pumpkin-and apple-picking make a good family outing. Go home with a bushel of apples to make applesauce and pies if your play is found in the kitchen, or use these ruby treasures for your Halloween apple-dunking game.

To carve an unusual jack-o-lantern this year, turn the pumpkin on its side and use its vine as its crook nose. Carve out eyes and a mouth to match.

Trip Tip: In 1991, the Rose Museum opened as part of Carnegie Hall's one hundredth anniversary celebration. The temporary exhibitions and the permanent collection document past concerts, lectures, and other events pertinent to America's musical and social history.

Schedule short trips around home, too. Sign up to learn how to make paper, participate in a poetry reading, or attend a free class at the local bike shop on how to repair a flat tire. Let your active and creative play be your pass to new adventures across town, the state, or the world.

Trip Tip: Plan a trip to visit a museum dedicated to your sport, hobby, or favorite artist or author. The Pedaling History Bicycle Museum in Orchard Park, New York, boasts the world's largest collection of antique and classic American bicycles.

FIELD TRIPS

Love the magic of live theater? Check out one of the best Shakespearean festivals in Ashland, Oregon. Call (541) 482-4331 for more information.

When your art hobby moves in with you permanently, start a list of museums to visit: Metropolitan Museum of Art, the Smithsonian, or the Louvre, and also include regional art shows and festivals, plus the changing shows at local galleries.

Travel solo, with a tour group, or a few like-minded friends to a new opening across the city. Take a sketchbook and attempt to recreate her still-life painting or sculpture. Plan to stay all day.

Trip Tip: When flying, drink tea to relax. Bring your stash of tea bags to ensure you have a flavor suited to your destination or frame of mind and body: blackberry sage offers a fruity taste, soft and sweet, with the fresh aroma of berries. This herbal tea has a balanced finish with a touch of sage. Honey ginseng is a delicious blend with ancient healthy properties of green tea. Ginger peach, a black tea with spicy ginger and the sweet lushness of fresh peach makes this hot or iced beverage a special treat for the weary traveler.

Write down the names of cities steeped in literary or musical history, and visit the birthplace and museums of authors and musicians. Travel to see your favorite band or singer, a theater or opera performance. By feeding your artistic spirit, you will keep your creative bank full.

Trip Tip: Every January, Elko, Nevada, hosts the world's largest gathering of cowboy poets.

New Orleans is a city saturated deep in the history of jazz and fine foods. Instead of filling up the thermos with a regular cup of joe, give what the locals drink here a try—coffee with a taste of chicory. Chicory, an herb which contains no calories or caffeine, can be roasted and ground in a manner similar to coffee, but some say chicory coffee is an acquired taste.

During the Civil War, chicory coffee was drunk south of the Mason-Dixon line supposedly because the North had cut off the South from its coffee bean supply. After the war though, southerners proudly adopted their own blends of coffee still flavored with chicory. Today, this popular cup of coffee is not complete without the region's donuts from the French Quarter—*beignets*, soft, square pillows of freshly baked dough sprinkled with powdered sugar and served hot. Even if you can't get chicory coffee and *beignets* locally, take a coffee-and-donut break and use the time to plan a trip.

Wolf Trap Foundation for the Performing Arts, located in Vienna, Virginia, offers various performances throughout the year. Call for upcoming events: (703) 255-1860.

I define "play" as getting away with a friend, fishing, and having a good time.
—*Gail Babb from Olean, New York*

Plan a vacation with several friends or your significant other to try a new sport or activity. Take the time—an extended weekend or an entire week—to elevate your fitness and mind to new heights. Put the trip on your calendar with enough time to prepare a base fitness level, especially if you are going to a high altitude.

Estes Park, Colorado, plays host to the Longs Peak Scottish Irish Highlands Festival September 5 through 8. The largest of its kind in North America with traditional food, games, music, seminars, and a parade. Call (800) 90-ESTES for more information. Afterwards, you can always hike next door in Rocky Mountain National Park.

Book with a tour group to learn how to whitewater raft, hang glide, or sea kayak. Head off to the mountains and learn to ski, cross-country ski, or snowshoe under the supervision of a qualified instructor. Attend a quilting workshop or a weekend meditation retreat. Sign up for a potter's workshop and turn the next weekend into a fun getaway dedicated to your new passion.

With a taste of experience, you may be prompted to pursue this new pastime after you return home.

Be Prepared

Running / Hiking: Carry a whistle or wear bells. Always take water, food, and a jacket if the weather should turn nasty.

Backpacking: Buy a good multipurpose tool like a Leatherman or Swiss Army knife.

Car Safety: Pack a flashlight, first aid kit, wool blankets, and water.

The main idea behind these excursions is to go for a reason besides relaxation. Promise to participate with both your feet and hands in order to include your active and creative self. Expect to be invigorated, stimulated, and refreshed at the end of your tours. The memories carried home will definitely be worth the price tag of any venture.

Trip Tip: Treat your musical ear this summer. July 13 through August 4 marks the annual celebration of Bach and other baroque composers in Carmel, California. These superb live performances sell out quickly: (831) 624-1521.

ROAD TRIPS

Car Aromatherapy: Citrus essences are uplifting and stimulating, perhaps a good replacement for another cup of coffee on a long road trip. Check your local health food store for a way to dispense grapefruit (citrus paradisi), lime (citrus aurantifolia), or mandarin (citrus reticulata) throughout the many miles of asphalt. Some retailers offer a plug-in device for the car's cigarette lighter or tiny ribbons soaked in the essence to be attached temporarily above the AC vent.

The world is a book, and those who do not travel read only a page.
—*Augustine (354–430)*

I am always looking for a new place to visit, another way to go to the same place if I must return. I clip travel articles, circle upcoming festivals, fairs, concerts, and any article that inspires me and provides yet another destination to visit. And I will go, if not this year, maybe next or at least by the time I am ninety-three. I file these interesting tidbits to guarantee future adventures and to provide my creative self with an endless supply of ideas from which to create, write, or imagine more about.

Trip Tip: The United States Boomerang Association hosts tournaments nationwide from Connecticut to Missouri to Washington.

For example, set out to discover what stands one hundred feet tall, weighs as much as one thousand five hundred mid-sized cars and was already two thousand years old when Columbus set sail. To see this beauty in person, plan a trip to the Giant Grove of Sequoia, Kings Canyon National Park, Northern California.

Or if you happen to be driving across the wide state of Texas, turn north on Interstate 40 and soak in 110 degree Fahrenheit natural hot springs, which lie beneath the small town of Truth or Consequences, New Mexico. For $7, you get a room to change in, a shower, a towel, and one of the most relaxing and best mineral bath soaks ever.

Traveling through the Carolinas? Return to the original spot of the Wright Brothers' first flight at Kitty Hawk, North Carolina. The warm, gentle breezes and the soft sand dunes of the Outer Banks will be the perfect place to learn how to hang glide. Key West, Florida, once home to Ernest Hemingway, boasts well-known artists and brand new names, scuba diving, snorkeling, and fishing that make this side trip worth the extra miles and hours in the car. Or, get on a boat and head off to Andros Island, bonefish capitol of the Bahamas.

For many miles in the car, you must have excellent music to get you there.
Bonnie Raitt's Road Tested *(double audio CD) just might do the job.*

Planning a trip to New York City? Get your walking shoes on because this thirteen-mile-long and two-mile-wide artist haven and international cuisine Mecca is waiting for your discovery. A walking tour of Manhattan, New York, will appease both your active and creative self as you pass through Little Italy, Chinatown, Soho, Greenwich Village, Gramercy Park, Midtown, and finally the Upper East or West Side and Harlem.

Start your own file for fun outings that encourages active or creative play. The fun part of this process is seeing how many new places you can travel to by year's end.

Trip Tip: Take Fido or Felix with you on your adventure. There are many lodging establishments that now welcome pets. Call ahead to confirm or research your options on line or at your local library.

DREAM VACATIONS

Twenty years from now you will be more disappointed by the things you didn't do than by the things you did. So, throw off the bowlines. Sail away from the safe harbor. Catch the trade winds in your sails. Explore. Dream. Discover.
—Mark Twain (1835–1910)

Let your dreams take you away and then earn you the means to do it again and again. Almost 150 years ago, a middle-aged Austrian woman named Ida Pfeiffer (1797–1858) took to international travel alone, alarming friends and family. She traveled to many distant ports and ancient cities of the world without much money or knowledge of the languages, oftentimes dressed in men's clothing for her own safety, but returned to write numerous books about her travels.

Another female adventurer, Rita Golden Gelman, is doing the same in the twenty-first century. To date, she has written more than seventy children's books and an adult tome, *Tales of a Female Nomad*.

You need only claim the events of your life to make yourself yours.
When you truly possess all you have been and done, which
may take some time, you are fierce with reality.
—Florida Scott Maxwell (1883–1978)

Pack your bags and your bikes for the Maah Daah Hey in North Dakota. This one
hundred-mile mountain bike trail runs through Theodore Roosevelt National Park
and is the longest continuous single track in the United States.

On a cross-country tour, make a detour to Detroit, Michigan, to tour the Motown Museum.

The rewards of the journey far outweigh the risk of leaving the harbor.
—Unknown

Vacations will never be the same old thing again.

Take to the roads to stimulate your imagination and move your body. It will make a world of difference in your life. Any amount of time spent indulging your new passion will restore your mind, body, and spirit. Now when you plan a weekend getaway trip or another family vacation, add a new element to your itinerary—play.

Include Play on Family Vacations

See the sights by walking, jogging, or bicycling.
Include hiking, backpacking, and/or swimming every day.
Dine al fresco. Pack a picnic and play lawn games afterwards.

In your travels, be on the lookout for new ideas. Your future adventures can be both a celebration of health and creativity with the added bonus to your happy times—the discovery of a new city or destination in nature. You will come home refreshed, re-energized, and ready for work and, of course, more fun.

Upon your return, you will be examining life from a new perspective because now you know the possibilities for exploratory play are without end. The world is awaiting your arrival—get packing.

Life is a marvelous, transitory adventure.
—Nikki Giovanni (b. 1943)

THE NEW NOVEL
BY WINSLOW HOMER

Books

A room without books is like a body without a soul.
—*Cicero (c.106–43 B.C.)*

Rest is as important as your days of play. If you miss a day or two—even a full week, your muscles will still remember how to move, stretch, and dance. You are not losing time, but gaining precious strength and endurance only achieved through giving your body and mind a break. When you step away from your art or hobby for a while, your return to it will be with new eyes.

Be sure to schedule this rest time regularly, and when you do, take one or two of these books with you. I think you will enjoy these authors' words.

ACTIVE PLAY

Climbing Free: My Life in the Vertical World by Lynn Hill with Greg Child

Game Face: What Does a Female Athlete Look Like? by Jane Gottesman

See How She Runs: Marion Jones & the Making of a Champion by Ron Rapoport

It's Not About The Bike: My Journey Back to Life by Lance Armstrong with Sally Jenkins

No Finish Line: My Life As I See It by Marla Runyan with Sally Jenkins

Outstanding Women Athletes: Who They Are and How They Influenced Sports in America
   by Janet Woolum

Picabo, Nothing to Hide by Picabo Street with Dana White

Riding for My Life by Julie Krone with Nancy Ann Richardson

Running and Walking for Women Over 40: The Road to Sanity and Vanity by Katherine Switzer

Surviving the Toughest Race on Earth by Martin Dugard

Women Who Win: Stories of Triumph in Sports and in Life by Christina Lessa

INSPIRATION

**There are two motives for reading a book; one, that you enjoy it;
the other, that you can boast about it.**
—*Bertrand Russell (1872–1970)*

A Short Guide to a Happy Life by Anna Quindlen

Deep Play by Diane Ackerman

Eat Mangoes Naked: Finding Pleasure Everywhere and Dancing with the Pits by SARK

Gift from the Sea by Anne Morrow Lindbergh

Imagine a Woman in Love With Herself: Embracing Your Wisdom and Wholeness by Patricia Lynn Reilly

The Promise of Wisdom by Kathy Wagoner

When You Eat at the Refrigerator, Pull Up a Chair: Fifty Ways to Feel Thin, Gorgeous & Happy by Geneen Roth

CREATIVE EXPRESSION

I have never known any distress that an hour's reading did not relieve.

—Charles Louis de Secondat, Baron de la Brede et de Montesquieu (1689–1755)

I Shock Myself: The Autobiography of Beatrice Wood by Beatrice Wood with Lindsay Smith

The Artist's Way: A Spiritual Path to Higher Creativity by Julia Cameron

The Knitting Goddess by Deborah Bergman

Writing Down the Bones: Freeing the Writer Within by Natalie Goldberg

ARMCHAIR TRAVEL

No entertainment is so cheap as reading, nor any pleasure so lasting.

—Lady M.W. Montague (1689–1762)

A Lady's Voyage Round the World by Ida Pfeiffer

Driving Over Lemons: An Optimist in Spain by Chris Stewart

Extra Virgin: A Young Woman Discovers the Italian Riviera, Where Every Month is Enchanted by
      Annie Hawes

French Dirt: The Story of a Garden in the South of France by Richard Goodman

Give Me the World by Leila Hadley

Solo: On Her Own Adventure edited by Susan Fox Rogers

Tales of a Female Nomad: Living at Large in the World by Rita Golden Gelman

FOR DAUGHTERS & GRANDDAUGHTERS

Books are the bees, which carry the quickening pollen from one to another mind.
—James Russell Lowell (1819–1891)

Hunger Pains: The Modern Woman's Tragic Quest for Thinness by Mary Pipher Ph.D.

Play Like A Girl: A Celebration of Women in Sports edited by Sue Macy and Jane Gottesman

Ophelia Speaks: Adolescent Girls Write About Their Search for Self by Sara Shandler

Go Girl!: Raising Healthy, Confident and Successful Girls through Sports by Hannah Storm with
Mark Jenkins

The Absolute Best Play Days: From Airplanes to Zoos (and Everything in Between!) by Pamela J.
      Waterman

The Beauty Myth: How Images of Beauty Are Used Against Women by Naomi Wolf

FUN AND GAMES

Choose an author as you choose a friend.

—Harper Lee (b. 1926)

Creative Puzzles of the World by Pieter Van Delft and Jack Botermans

Hoyle's Rules of Games by Edmond Hoyle

The Oxford History of Board Games by David Parlett

The Simple Solution to Rubik's Cube by James G. Nourse

PERMISSIONS

p. xii *Ecstasy*, 1929 (oil on board) by Maxfield Parrish (1870–1966)
Private Collection, Cornish Colony Gallery & Museum, from the archives
of Alma Gilbert

p.10 *A Lady with Lyre* (panel) by Charles Edward Halle (1846–1914)
Phillips, The International Fine Art Auctioneers, UK/Bridgeman Art Library

p.22 *The Favourite*, 1901 by John William Godward (1861–1922), Richard Green,
London

p.38 *A Boating Party*, 1889 (oil on canvas) by John Singer Sargent (1856–1925)
Museum of Art, Rhode Island School of Design; Gift of Mrs. Houghton P. Metcalf
in memory of her husband, Houghton P. Metcalf

p.56 *Tennis Players*, 1885 by Horace Henry Cauty (1846–1909)
Christopher Wood Gallery, London, UK/Bridgeman Art Library

p.88 *The Music Lesson*, 1877 (oil on canvas) by Lord Frederic Leighton (1830–1896)
Guildhall Art Gallery, Corporation of London, UK/Bridgeman Art Library

p.110 *The Cheat with the Ace of Clubs* (oil on canvas) by Georges de La Tour (1593–1652) Kimbell Art Museum, Fort Worth, Texas, USA/Bridgeman Art Library

p.126 *Family in the Orchard*, 1890 by Theo van Rysselberghe (1862–1926) Rijksmuseum Kroller-Muller, Otterlo, Netherlands/Bridgeman Art Library

p. 144 *Little Girl Skiing*, by Carl Larsson (1853–1919) Private Collection/Bridgeman Art Library

p.164 *Boating on the Seine*, c.1879 (oil on canvas) by Pierre Auguste Renoir (1841–1919) National Gallery, London, UK/Bridgeman Art Library

p.182 *The New Novel*, by Winslow Homer (1836–1910) Museum of Fine Arts, Horace P. Wright Collection

ABOUT THE AUTHOR

Jill Murphy Long has been playing all of her life. As a little tyke, she painted, sketched, threw clay around, and baked candy stained glass windows with her artist mother. She climbed trees, built tree houses, and played baseball with her brother and the neighborhood boys. Active and creative play abounded around the little house in rural Pennsylvania with all of the typical backyard summertime games: badminton, croquet, and water fun, plus frequent doll and art shows and scavenger hunts. Wintertime brought out the board games and craft projects for many hours of laughs and creative expression.

At sixteen, she learned how to alpine ski, and she raced during college. In her twenties, she raced on her road bike, and in her thirties switched to competing on her mountain bike. Not much has changed in the last four decades, except the addition of new fun and games for the author. She and her husband tried hang gliding on their honeymoon and hot air ballooning for their first year wedding anniversary. Jill put on her first pair of snowshoes at thirty-seven and is still trying to learn how to cross-country ski and snowboard well. Every summer, she pulls out her cycling, hiking, camping, and tennis gear. Throughout the year, this amateur artist is always dabbling in paints on the wall or on paper, creating handmade crafts, and appreciating the arts whenever she can.

As a former advertising executive and Professional Ski Instructor of America (PSIA), Jill is now a certified yoga instructor and member of Wombats (Women on Mountain Bikes and Tea Society) and the International Mountain Bike Association (IMBA). She still reserves time for fun as an Ambassador for the Steamboat Ski Resort between her book tours, research, and writing. A self-proclaimed bibliophile, she belongs to a reading club and has organized and led weekly writers' groups. Jill and her family live in Steamboat Springs, Colorado, where adults and kids play every day.